新双双中文教材 10
New Chinese Language and Culture Course

中国古代科学技术 Ancient Chinese Science and Technology

（第二版）

[美] 王双双　编著

张罗蕴　画

图书在版编目（CIP）数据

中国古代科学技术/（美）王双双编著. —2版.—北京：北京大学出版社，2020.8
新双双中文教材
ISBN 978-7-301-31463-0

Ⅰ.①中… Ⅱ.①王… Ⅲ.①汉语—对外汉语教学—教材 ②自然科学史—中国—古代 Ⅳ.①H195.4

中国版本图书馆CIP数据核字（2020）第145567号

书　　　　名	中国古代科学技术（第二版） ZHONGGUO GUDAI KEXUE JISHU（DI-ER BAN）
著作责任者	［美］王双双　编著
英文翻译	［德］Nanny Kim（金兰中）
责任编辑	邓晓霞
标准书号	ISBN 978-7-301-31463-0
出版发行	北京大学出版社
地　　　　址	北京市海淀区成府路205号　100871
网　　　　址	http://www.pup.cn　　　新浪微博：@北京大学出版社
电子信箱	zpup@pup.cn
电　　　　话	邮购部 010-62752015　发行部 010-62750672　编辑部 010-62753334
印刷者	北京宏伟双华印刷有限公司
经销者	新华书店
	889毫米×1194毫米　16开本　11.75印张　236千字
	2007年5月第1版
	2020年8月第2版　2022年9月第2次印刷
定　　　　价	88.00元（含课本、练习本、音频）

未经许可，不得以任何方式复制或抄袭本书之部分或全部内容。
版权所有，侵权必究
举报电话：010-62752024　电子信箱：fd@pup.pku.edu.cn
图书如有印装质量问题，请与出版部联系，电话：010-62756370

第二版序

能够与北京大学出版社合作出版"双双中文教材"的第二版，让这套优秀的对外汉语教材泽被更多的学生，加州中文教学研究中心倍感荣幸。

这是一套洋溢着浓浓爱意的教材。作者的女儿在美国出生，到了识字年龄，作者教她学习过市面上流行的多套中文教材，但都强烈地感觉到这些教材"水土不服"。一解女儿学习中文的燃眉之急，是作者编写这套教材的初衷和原动力。为了让没有中文环境的孩子能够喜欢学习中文，作者字斟句酌地编写课文；为了赋予孩子审美享受、引起他们的共鸣，作者特邀善画儿童创作了一幅幅稚气可爱的插图；为了加深孩子们对内容的理解，激发孩子们的学习热情，作者精心设计了充满创造性的互动活动。

这是一套承载着文化传承使命感的教材。语言不仅仅是文化的载体，更是文化重要的有机组成部分。学习一门外语的深层障碍往往根植于目标语言与母语间的文化差异。这种差异对于学习中文的西方学生尤为突出。这套教材的使用对象正处在好奇心和好胜心最强的年龄阶段，作者抓住了这一特点，变阻力为动力，一改过去削学生认知能力和智力水平之"足"以适词汇和语言知识之"履"的通病。教材在高年级部分，一个学期一个文化主题，以对博大精深的中国文化的探索激发学生的学习兴趣，使学生在学习语言的同时了解璀璨的中国文化。

"双双中文教材"自2005年面世以来，受到了老师、学生和家长的广泛欢迎。很多觉得中文学习枯燥无味而放弃的学生，因这套教材发现了学习中文的乐趣，又重新回到了中文课堂。本次修订，作者不仅吸纳了老师们对于初版的反馈意见和自己实际使用过程中的心得，还参考了近年对外汉语教学理论及实践方面的成果。语言学习部分由原来的九册改为五册，一学年学习一册，文化学习部分保持一个专题一册。相信修订后的"新双双中文教材"会更方便、实用，让更多学生受益。

张晓江

美国加州中文教学研究中心秘书长

第一版前言

"双双中文教材"是一套专门为海外青少年编写的中文课本，是我在美国八年的中文教学实践基础上编写成的。在介绍这套教材之前，请读一首小诗：

> 一双神奇的手，
> 推开一扇窗。
> 一条神奇的路，
> 通向灿烂的中华文化。

鲍凯文　鲍维江

鲍维江和鲍凯文姐弟俩是美国生美国长的孩子，也是我的学生。1998年冬，他们送给我的新年贺卡上的小诗，深深地打动了我的心。我把这首诗看成我文化教学的"回声"。我要传达给海外每位中文老师：我教给他们（学生）中国文化，他们思考了、接受了、回应了。这条路走通了！

语言是一种交流的工具，更是一种文化和一种生活方式，所以学习中文也就离不开中华文化的学习。汉字是一种古老的象形文字，她从远古走来，带有大量的文化信息，但学起来并不容易。使学生增强兴趣、减小难度，走出苦学汉字的怪圈，走进领悟中华文化的花园，是我编写这套教材的初衷。

学生不论大小，天生都有求知的欲望，都有欣赏文化美的追求。中华文化本身是魅力十足的。把这宏大而玄妙的文化，深入浅出地，有声有色地介绍出来，让这迷人的文化如涓涓细流，一点一滴地渗入学生们的心田，使学生们逐步体味中国文化，是我编写这套教材的目的。

为此我将汉字的学习放入文化介绍的流程之中同步进行，让同学们在学中国地理的同时，学习汉字；在学中国历史的同时，学习汉字；在学中国哲学的同时，学习汉字；在学中国科普文选的同时，学习汉字……

这样的一种中文学习，知识性强，趣味性强；老师易教，学生易学。当学生们合上书本时，他们的眼前是中国的大好河山，是中国五千年的历史和妙不可言的哲学思维，是奔腾的现代中国……

总之，他们了解了中华文化，就会探索这片土地，热爱这片土地，就会与中国结下情缘。

最后我要衷心地感谢所有热情支持和帮助我编写教材的老师、家长、学生、朋友和家人。特别是老同学唐玲教授、何茜老师和我女儿Uta Guo年复一年的鼎力相助。可以说这套教材是大家努力的结果。

王双双

课程设置（建议）

序号	书名	适用年级
1	中文课本　第一册	幼儿园/一年级
2	中文课本　第二册	二年级
3	中文课本　第三册	三年级
4	中文课本　第四册	四年级
5	中文课本　第五册	五年级
6	中国成语故事	六年级
7	中国地理常识	六年级
8	中国古代故事	七年级
9	中国神话传说	七年级
10	中国古代科学技术	八年级
11	中国民俗与民间艺术	八年级
12	中国文学欣赏	九年级
13	中国诗歌欣赏	九年级
14	中国古代哲学	十年级
15	中国历史	十年级

目录

第一课　四大发明（一）指南针 …………… 1

第二课　四大发明（二）蔡伦造纸 ………… 11

第三课　四大发明（三）火药 ……………… 20

第四课　四大发明（四）活字印刷术 ……… 29

第五课　丝　绸 ……………………………… 39

第六课　李春造桥 …………………………… 51

第七课　扁鹊的四诊法 ……………………… 60

第八课　李时珍和他的《本草纲目》……… 71

第九课　都江堰 ……………………………… 83

第十课　中国瓷器 …………………………… 94

选修课　张衡和他的地动仪 ………………… 105

生字表（简） ………………………………… 111

生字表（繁） ………………………………… 113

生词表（简） ………………………………… 115

生词表（繁） ………………………………… 117

附录 "新双双中文教材"写作练习（1—10册）… 119

洪涛　冯聪英　画

第一课

四大发明（一）
指南针

这是一把汤勺吗？不是。这是一块棋盘吗？不是。这是中国古老的指南针。

大约在2,000多年前的战国时期，中国人就发现磁石可以用来指方向。他们把天然磁石磨成一个光滑的小勺，放在一个写有方位的盘子上，让它自由转动。盘子又平又滑，勺子停下来的时候，勺把指的方向总是南方，这就是最早的指南针，当时叫司南。

王金泰　画

1,000多年前，中国人又发明了"指南鱼"。指南鱼是用2寸长、5分①宽的薄铁片做成一条鱼的形状，鱼肚部分凹下去一些，可以像小船一样浮在水面上；然后进行人工磁化，就是把铁片与天然磁石放在一起紧紧地挨着，时间久了，铁片就有了磁性。这样，只要有一碗水，把指南鱼放在水面上，就可以指示南北方向了。

可是指南鱼的磁性有时太弱，不太好用。后来人们把一根钢针放在磁石上磨，使钢针变成了磁针。磁针穿上几根干草，就可以浮在水面指示方向。还有一种方法是用一根细线把磁针挂在没有风的地方，下面配有写着方位的盘，磁针和盘一起组成了真正的指南针。这就是可以准确指示方向的罗盘。

到了12世纪（北宋），中国的海船上就装有罗盘。这样不管是白天还是黑夜，阴雨还是大雾，船都不会迷失方向，使海上航行安全多了。

13世纪初（南宋），中国的指南针传到欧洲，大大促进了世界航海业的发展。

---

① 分——长度单位，10分等于1寸。

第一课

生词

tāng sháo 汤勺	spoon, ladle	pèi 配	equip, fit
cí 磁	magnetic	luó pán 罗盘	Luopan, compass
fāng wèi 方位	position	shì jì 世纪	century
zì yóu 自由	freely, with freedom	wù 雾	fog
báo 薄	thin	mí shī 迷失	get lost
tiě 铁	iron	ān quán 安全	safe
āo 凹	concave	chū 初	beginning
āi 挨	be near, place next to	cù jìn 促进	advance
zhǐ shì 指示	direct	háng hǎi 航海	navigation
gāng 钢	steel		

听写

汤勺　磁　方位　自由　铁　钢　罗盘　雾

迷失　安全　初　航海　*配　促进

注：*号以后的字词为选做题，后同。

比一比

| 雨 | 雪 | 雷 | 雾 |

$\begin{cases} 雨（下雨）\\ 雾（下雾）\end{cases}$ $\begin{cases} 雪（白雪）\\ 雷（打雷）\end{cases}$

$\begin{cases} 足（足球）\\ 促（促进）\end{cases}$ 航$\begin{cases} 航行\\ 航空\\ 航海\end{cases}$

| 司南 | 司机 | 公司 |

反义词

薄——厚　　　　　　　　天然——人工

词语运用

促进

① 画画儿能促进一个人的想象力。

② 给竹子上肥,可以促进竹子生长。

③ 回收垃圾,可以促进环保。

不管……还是……

① 不管白天还是黑夜,医院里都有医生在工作。

② 今年夏天不管你去还是不去中国,我是要去的。

③ 不管阴天还是大雾,有了指南针海船就安全多了。

阅读

磁石的故事

秦始皇统一了中国,建立秦朝(前221—前206)。他建造了一个大宫殿。在一个夜晚,有一些人想刺杀他,这些人身上背着宝剑跳墙进入皇宫。他们往前走,看见一个大门,正想进去,突然一个身上背宝剑的人被大门吸住,不能动了!另一个手拿宝剑的人想帮助他，谁知道宝剑也被大门吸住了。原来这个宫门是磁石做的，身上带着武器(wǔ)的人是不能通过的。这几个人只好丢掉宝剑逃跑了。

洪涛　冯聪英　画

资料

磁石与人工磁化

春秋战国时期，人们在寻矿(kuàng)时，常会遇到磁石，很早就知道磁石吸铁的特性，并记载(zǎi)在书里①。那时的人称"磁"为"慈"，他们把磁石吸引铁看作慈母对子女的吸引。

古时，人工磁化的方法之一，是将铁片放在火中烧，烧红的铁片放在子午线的方向上，这时，铁片内部分子处于活动状态，铁分子顺着地球磁场方向排列(liè)，达到磁化目的。

指南鱼

宋代，人们发明了"指南鱼"。有一种"指南鱼"是用木头做的。鱼肚子里放上一块磁石，S极朝外，鱼嘴里插一根针。这样把鱼放进一碗水里，鱼嘴里的针，指的方向总是南方。

---

① 《管子》一书中最早记载："山上有磁石者，其下有金铜。"
《吕氏春秋》中有："慈(cí)招铁，或引之也。"

沈括和《梦溪笔谈》

宋代科学家沈括,在《梦溪笔谈》中描述了如何把磁化的钢针做成指南针和四种指南的方法。他还发现了"磁偏角",也就是说,指南针的磁极与地球的南极、北极有一点儿偏差。

①水浮(水磁针)　②放在指甲上

③放在碗边　　　　④用细线悬挂磁针

洪涛　冯聪英　画

小实验:古代人将钢针人工磁化做成磁针,你想试试吗?

Lesson One

The Four Great Inventions, Part 1
The Compass

Is this a ladle? Is it a chess board? No, it's an ancient Chinese compass.

Over two thousand years ago in the Warring States period, Chinese people discovered that loadstones could show the direction. They worked a natural magnetic stone into a smooth small ladle and placed it on a flat board with markings for the directions so that it could turn freely. When the ladle came to a halt on the flat and shiny board, its handle would always point south, so it was the earliest "south pointing needle" or, at the time, the "south director".

More than a thousand years ago, Chinese invented the "south pointing fish". They shaped a thin piece of iron into a fish that was 2 inches long and 0.5 inch wide with the "belly" slightly bent inwards so that it could swim on water like a little boat. The iron was then magnetized by placing it next to a loadstone for a long time. After that, all you needed was a bowl of water. When you placed your "south pointing fish" on it, it would point south.

However, the magnetism of the "south pointing fish" was sometimes weak, making the device unreliable. Later on, people used a steel needle and magnetized it by rubbing it against loadstones. The needle was then placed inside several straws, so that it would swim on water and show directios. Another way was to hang the needle on a thin thread in a windless place, with a dial underneath that show bearings. In this way the hanging needle and the dial form a true compass. This is Luopan that can give the right directions.

By the twelfth century (the Northern Song), Chinese seagoing ships used this Luopan. No matter day or night, rain or fog, the ships no longer lost directions, and navigation thus became much safer.

In the early thirteenth century (the Southern Song), the Chinese compass came to Europe, providing a major advance in navigation.

Stories about Loadstones

Qin Shihuang united China and founded the Qin dynasty (221-206 BC). He built a great palace. There were some people who wanted to assassinate him; and one night, they strapped swords to their backs and climbed over the walls into the imperial palace. They came to a great door and were just about to enter it, when one man's sword stuck to the door and the man found himself immobilized. Another came to help, yet his sword, too, was stuck to the door. This palace door was made from loadstone, so that people carrying weapons could not pass. The disarmed attackers had to run away.

Loadstones and Artificial Magnetization

In the Spring and Autumn and the Warring States periods, people often found loadstones when prospecting for ores. They early on realized that the loadstone attracted irons and wrote this down[①]. At the time the character used for "magnetism" was "kindness". They regarded the magnet's attraction to iron as that of a loving mother to her children.

In antiquity, artificial magnetization was performed by placing iron flakes in a fire until they became red hot, and then arranging them along a meridian. Under great heat, the molecules in the iron became mobile, and arranged themselves along the meridian, acquiring directivity. Thus the iron became magnetic.

The South Pointing Fish

The invention of the "south pointing fish" dates to the Song period. One kind of "south pointing fish" was made from wood. A magnet was placed in the belly of the fish, with its S pole pointing outwards. A needle was put into the fish's mouth. Then, put the fish in a bowl of water and the needle in its mouth would always point south.

Shen Kuo and his *Mengxibitan*

In his book *The Dream Pool Essays*, the Song scientist Shen Kuo described how steel needles could be magnetized and made into compasses as well as four ways of using the south pointing needles. He also discovered the magnetic deviation; the fact that the direction indicated by the compass slightly deviates from the exact south or north.

---

① *Guanzi* records: Where loadstone is found on a mountain, gold and copper are found in the ground.
Lüshi Chunqiu records: Ci [loadstone] summons iron, it may be used as a guide.

第二课

四大发明（二）
蔡伦造纸

中国古代，在没有发明纸以前，人们大多把文字写在竹简上。

竹简很笨重，不方便，有的官员写一份报告给皇帝，要由两个人吃力地抬进宫去。那时，还有人用帛写字。帛是丝织品，很轻便，但是非常贵，要用720斤大米才能换一匹帛，一般人根本用不起。

西汉时已有人开始用丝絮和麻造纸，但这种麻纸很粗糙。东汉时有个叫蔡伦的人，想要造出一种更好的纸，给人们写字。他看到人们把蚕茧煮熟后放在席子上，再放到河里，用棍子敲打成烂丝绵，当把丝绵揭下来时，席子上会留下一层薄薄的絮片。絮片晒干揭下来就能在上面写字了。虽然丝絮片无法大量生产，但是这个方法让蔡伦想到树皮、麻头、旧渔网和破布等可以做原料。他做了很多试验，把树皮、麻头、旧渔网和破布一起煮成浆，再放在席子上，刮成薄薄一层，放在太阳底下晒干。这就是那时候世界上最好的纸。在这种纸上写字又吃墨又光滑，十分理想。

公元105年，蔡伦把这一重大发现报告给皇帝。因为这样造出的纸又轻又便宜又好用，人们都很喜欢，所以全国的人很快就都用上了这种纸。

造纸术在几百年后传到了朝鲜、日本、印度、阿拉伯和欧洲，促进了世界文化的发展。

王金泰　画

生词

cài lún 蔡伦	Cai Lun	jiē 揭	remove, tear off
zhú jiǎn 竹简	bamboo slips	shēng chǎn 生产	produce
bèn zhòng 笨重	cumbersome, heavy	yú wǎng 渔网	fishing net
bào gào 报告	report	pò bù 破布	rag
bó 帛	silk gauze	yuán liào 原料	raw materials
sī xù 丝絮	silk wadding	shì yàn 试验	experiment
má 麻	hemp	jiāng 浆	pulp
cū cāo 粗糙	coarse	mò 墨	ink
gùn zi 棍子	stick	lǐ xiǎng 理想	ideal
sī mián 丝绵	silk floss	ā lā bó 阿拉伯	Arabia

听写

竹简　笨重　报告　帛　粗糙　棍子　揭　生产

破布　原料　试验　浆　墨　阿拉伯　*蔡伦

13

比一比

布 { 分布 / 棉布 }　　料 { 原料 / 布料 }　　简 { 竹简 / 简单 }

看看下面字词的组成，有哪些相同之处，为什么？

[布 / 帛]　　　　[帛 / 丝绵]　　　　[丝绵 / 纸]

反义词

破烂——完好　　　　便宜——贵

笨重——轻便　　　　粗糙——精细

多音字

pián	biàn
便	便
便宜	方便　轻便
这双球鞋很便宜。	有了手机，生活方便了很多。
	纸比竹简轻便多了。

词语运用

生产

① 这是一家生产电动汽车的公司。

② 东汉蔡伦改进了造纸术,并开始大量生产纸。

③ 这家毛笔厂生产的毛笔很有名。

试验

① 蔡伦用树皮、旧渔网等做了很多次试验,才造出纸。

② 奶奶爱做试验,常常做出不同味道的点心。

③ 妹妹是个爱动手做试验的人。

词语解释

笨重——又大又重

思考题

现在有手机、电脑,字可以显示在屏幕上,再往后字会显示在哪里?

阅读

（一）

古代，没有纸以前，人们把文字写在哪里？

古代，苏美尔人在泥版上刻写文字。

古代，埃及人在莎(suō)草纸上写字。

古代，印度人在贝叶上写字。

古代，欧洲人在羊皮纸上写字。

那古代中国人把字写在哪儿呢？

古苏美尔人在泥版上刻写文字。

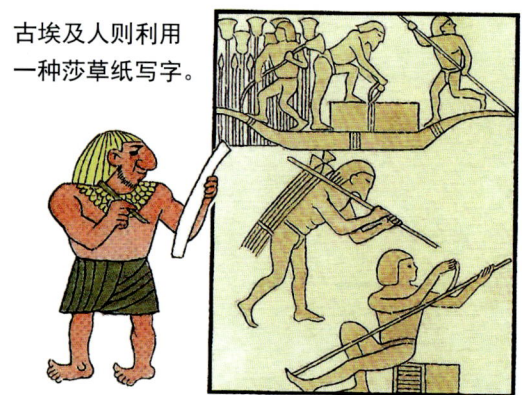
古埃及人则利用一种莎草纸写字。

古印度人在贝叶上写字。

古代欧洲人把文字记录在羊皮纸上。

洪涛　冯聪英　画

（二）

从甲骨到纸张

人类有了文字，就要书写。在没有纸之前，中国人把字写在哪儿呢？有许多书写材料：将字刻在龟甲、兽骨上的，是甲骨文；将字铸造在青铜器上的，是金文；将字刻在石头上的，叫碑(bēi)文；也有写在竹简上的，写在布帛上的。在龟甲上刻字，在石头上刻字，把字铸造在青铜器上，都很不容易，也不方便携(xié)带，写在帛上又太贵。公元105年，汉朝的蔡伦改进了造纸术，使纸变得又便宜又方便又好用，从此代替了竹简和帛。随后，纸图书也就出现了。中国有句古话"纸寿千年"，是说传统造纸技术造出的古纸，可保存千年。

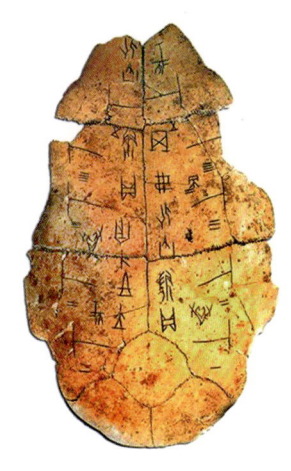

甲骨文

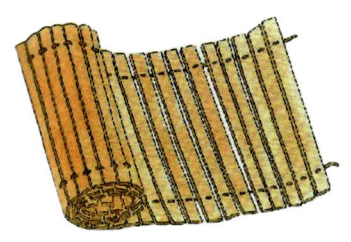

Lesson Two

The Four Great Inventions, Part 2
Cai Lun, the Inventor of Papermaking

In Chinese antiquity before the invention of paper, bamboo slips were the ordinary writing materials. Bamboo slips are cumbersome. Sometimes, the report that an official submitted to the emperor required two men to carry! At the time, silk gauze was also used as a writing material. This material is light, but expensive. 720 *jin* of rice only bought a single bolt of silk gauze, so this was out of reach for ordinary people.

In the Western Han, people began making paper from wads of raw silk and hemp, but this paper was coarse. In the Eastern Han, Cai Lun thought about a better kind of paper that could be used for writing. He watched silk makers cooking the silkworms, placing them on mats, then lowering these in the river and beating the cocoons into silk floss. They ripped the silk floss off, and wads of raw silk were left on the mats. When dried, these wads could serve as writing materials. However, there was no way of producing these patches in larger quantities. Cai Lun therefore thought about alternative raw materials, such as bark, hemp, old fishing nets, or rags. Through much experimenting, he found a mixture of these four materials that he cooked into a pulp and spread on a mat, then skimmed into a thin layer and dried under the sun. The result was the best paper available worldwide at the time. It was ideal for it absorbed some ink yet and offered a smooth surface.

In 105 AD, Cai Lun reported his invention to the emperor. Because paper thus produced was light, cheap and convenient in every respect, people liked it and it soon was used all over China.

In the following centuries, papermaking spread to Korea, Japan, India, Arabia, and Europe, greatly advancing cultural development.

(I)

In antiquity, before the invention of paper, what did people write on?
The ancient Sumerians wrote on clay tablets.
The ancient Egyptians wrote on papyrus.
The ancient Indians wrote on pattra leaves.
The ancient Europeans wrote on pergament.
What did the ancient Chinese write on?

(II)
From Tortoise Shells and Bones to Paper

Once characters had been invented, people wanted to write things down. But what did Chinese write on before the invention of paper? They used many materials: They cut characters into tortoise shells or bones (oracle bone script), they cast them into bronze objects (bronze script), they cut them into stone tablets (inscription script), and they wrote on bamboo slips and on silk. Cutting into bones and stones as well as bronzes were difficult technologies, and silk was very expensive. In 105 AD, Cai Lun improved the paper making. Then paper became cheap and convenient, so it replaced bamboo slips and silk. Soon, paper books appeared. There is a Chinese saying "paper survives a thousand years", and in fact traditionally produced paper can last this long.

第三课

四大发明（三）

火药

人人都喜欢烟花，喜欢闪闪的华光，喜欢色彩缤^{bīn}纷的夜空。在中国，春节的夜晚，很多地方都可以看到快乐的孩子们放烟花和爆竹，砰^{pēng}—砰！啪^{pā}—啪！在烟花和爆竹声中，迎来新的一年。

烟花和爆竹是用什么做成的呢？是用火药做的。中国是世界上最早发明火药的国家。

王金泰　画

那火药又是怎样发明的呢？说来有趣，火药的发明，要先从炼丹说起。在古代中国，人们都想长生不老，特别是皇帝。许多炼丹术士，梦想炼出让人长生不老的仙药。他们不断地找来各种矿石和植物，在炼丹炉中试验。试

验是危险的，有时炼丹炉会突然发出爆炸声，冒出大火把房子烧了。经过一次次的爆炸起火，人们终于发现：把硫(liú)黄、硝(xiāo)石、木炭这三样东西，按照一定的比例混合在一起加热，就会爆炸。这就是火药。结果仙药没有炼出，却意外地发明了火药。火药发明的时间大约在1,500年前（唐朝）。

自从有了火药，人类得到了一种前所未有的巨大力量。很快，火药就被用在武器上。不久，中国人发明了火药箭。在宋朝，一次作战就用了25万只火药箭。宋朝政府有了火药作坊，不断发明各种火器：比如"火球"，点着后升空，爆炸时就像打雷，还飞出大量石灰迷住敌人的眼睛；又比如"突(tōng)火枪"，就是把火药装在竹筒里，再放上像"子弹"一样的小铁块、小石子。这是世界上最早的"枪"。同时火药还被用来开山采矿、做成烟花爆竹，供人们过节使用。

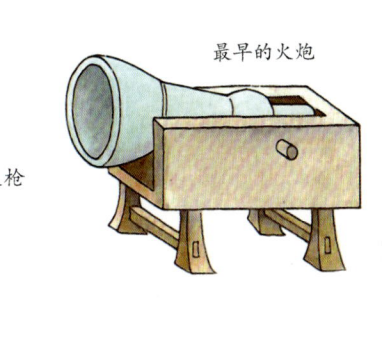

最早的火炮

突火枪

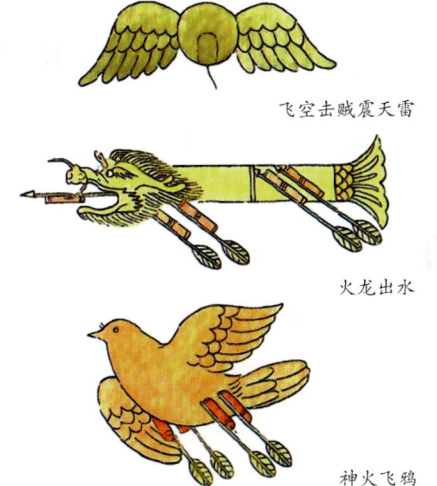

飞空击贼震天雷

火龙出水

神火飞鸦

13世纪，火药传入印度，后来又传入阿拉伯和欧洲。

生词

huǒ yào 火药	gunpowder, explosive	yì wài 意外	unexpectedly
yān huā 烟花	fireworks	qián suǒ wèi yǒu 前所未有	unprecedented
liàn dān 炼丹	concoct pills of immortality	lì liàng 力量	force
kuàng 矿	mining	wǔ qì 武器	weapon
lú 炉	stove	zuò zhàn 作战	combat
bào zhà 爆炸	explode	zhèng fǔ 政府	government
mù tàn 木炭	charcoal	zuō fang 作坊	workshop
àn zhào 按照	according to	qiāng 枪	gun
bǐ lì 比例	proportion	zǐ dàn 子弹	bullet
hùn hé 混合	mix	gōng 供	provide, supply

听写

火药　矿　爆炸　按照　比例　混合　前所未有

力量　武器　政府　枪　供　*烟花　子弹

比一比

量 { 力量
     商量

混（混合）
棍（木棍）

炸（爆炸）
昨（昨天）
作（作业）

| 作 | 昨 | 炸 |

作业　　昨天　　爆炸

反义词

意外——故意

多音字

zuò
作
作战　作业

zuō
作
作坊

词语运用

比例

① 这个学校男生和女生的比例是3∶2。

② 这个人的头画得太大，比例不合适。

③ 做这种面包，面和水的比例是2∶1。

按照

① 我按照老师的要求把课文大声读了两遍。

② 居民们按照要求，把垃圾分类放在不同的桶里。

③ 奶奶按照医生的建议，每天走路半小时。

意外

① 我回家时，遇到了意外，车被追尾了。

② 不出意外的话，飞机应该已经落地了。

③ 飞机的挡风玻璃意外破裂了，机长竟然把飞机安全飞回来了。

词语解释

爆竹——鞭炮，中国用于传统节日、婚礼等喜庆活动上

术士——多指道教中以炼丹为职业的人

阅读

炼丹与火药

和尚喜欢念经，道士热心炼丹，炼呀，炼呀，炼出了吓人的火药。

中国古代有许多道士，梦想炼石成金，或炼出长生不老的仙丹。他们找来各种矿石和植物，进行着艰苦又危险的试验。硝石、硫黄在古时候被认为是药材，马兜铃经过燃烧变成了木炭。

徐心怡　画

道士本想炼丹做药，但这三样东西放在一起就是火药——"可以着火的药"。有时炼丹炉会起火爆炸。后来人们逐渐掌握了硝石、硫黄和木炭的比例，仙药没有炼成，火药问世了。

勇敢的万户

自古以来，人们就梦想飞上天空。14世纪（明朝），中国有一位万户，他想火药能把箭送上天，要是把很多的火药绑在椅子上，一定能把人送上天。于是他在椅子后面装了许多火药，自己坐在椅子上，两手各拿着一个大风筝，想先飞上天空，再靠风筝慢慢飘下来。他让人点火，一声爆炸后，他摔了下来。万户虽然没有成功，但他的想法是有道理的。600多年后，人们借助火箭飞上了天空。

Lesson Three

The Four Great Inventions, Part 3
Gunpowder

Everybody loves fireworks, the sparks and the colors in the sky. In China, on the night of the Spring Festival, children let off fireworks and firecrackers in many places. Bang, Bang! The racket and the glitter welcome the New Year.

What are firecrackers made of? They contain gunpowder. And gunpowder was invented in China.

How were explosives discovered? Interestingly, this has to do with alchemy. In ancient China, people wished for never-ending youth, especially the emperors. Many alchemists pursued their dream of finding the elixir of life. They explored minerals and plants and made experiments on their alchemist stoves. These experiments could be dangerous; sometimes the substances ignited and burnt the house down. Through many explosive experiments, they found out that mixing sulphur, phosphorous and charcoal in certain proportions made a powder that exploded when ignited, and this became the gunpowder. The alchemists never discovered the elixir of immortality, but they invented explosives. This was about 1,500 years ago in the Tang period.

Gunpowder was soon employed to make in weapons and equipped armies with new military power. Chinese soon invented weapons loaded with gunpowder that shot out arrows. In the Song period, some 250,000 arrow guns were used in warfare. The Song government maintained specialized gunpowder workshops and developed new weapons, such as "fireballs", which flew up after ignition and exploded in mid-air like a thunderclap, dropping dust and grit to blind the enemies. Another weapon was the "Tu Huo Qiang", in which gunpowder was put in a bamboo tube, and then small pieces of iron or stone that were like "bullets" were put in it. This was the first "gun". At the same time, explosives were also used in mining and for firecrackers, becoming part of festivals.

In the thirteenth century, gunpowder was transmitted to India, and somewhat later to Arabia and to Europe.

Alchemy and Gunpowder

Buddhist monks devoted themselves to reciting sutras; Taoists enthused about brewing magic pills. Their brewing and concocting eventually led to a fearful invention: Explosives.

In Chinese antiquity, Taoist alchemists were numerous, and their dream was transforming stone to gold or finding the elixir of life. They found many minerals and plants and experimented with them, undeterred by dangers and hardships. Saltpeter and sulphur were regarded as drug ingredients, and the Chinese aristolochia, a peculiar-looking flower, was burnt to charcoal. An experiment intended to produce a magic drug that used these three ingredients led to a "fire drug". Occasionally, a stove exploded during these experiments. Later on, with better understanding of the proportions of the ingredients, it became clear that this was no medication, but the invention of gunpowder.

The Courageous Wan Hu

Forever, people have been dreaming of flying up in the sky. In the fourteenth century during the Ming period, there was an official named Wan Hu who thought that if gunpowder could shoot arrows into the sky, it might send a man flying if he was tied to a chair. So he had large amounts of gunpowder attached to the back of a chair, then sat down on it, holding two large kites, one in each hand. The plan was to be shot up into the air and glide down with the help of the kites. He had the gunpowder lighted, and crashed down to the ground in a great explosion. He failed in his attempt to fly, yet he had grasped a workable principle. More than 600 years later, humanity realized his dream in manned rockets.

第四课

四大发明（四）
活字印刷术

中国古代在印刷术发明以前，书要一个字一个字地用手抄写，速度很慢。

唐朝中期，人们发明了雕版印刷术，就是用刀把书上的字，一笔一笔地

刻在一块硬木上，再印刷。雕版印刷比起用手抄写，不知快了多少。但是每块雕版上的字都是固定的，每换一次内容，就得重刻一次版，很不方便。

12世纪（北宋），有一个叫毕升的人，发明了活字印刷术。

毕升小时候因为家里穷，只读了几年书，就到一家印书的作坊里去做工匠。毕升的工作非常辛苦，一天到晚要整版整版地刻字。可是刻字时，一笔刻坏了，整块版就作废了，这可怎么办呢？于是他想了

个办法，把刻坏的字挖去，再刻一个字补进去。这个办法真是太好了。这使毕升想到，如果用一块块的小木头，刻成单个字，用时排在一起，不用时再拆开，留着下次用。这不是又简单又方便吗？

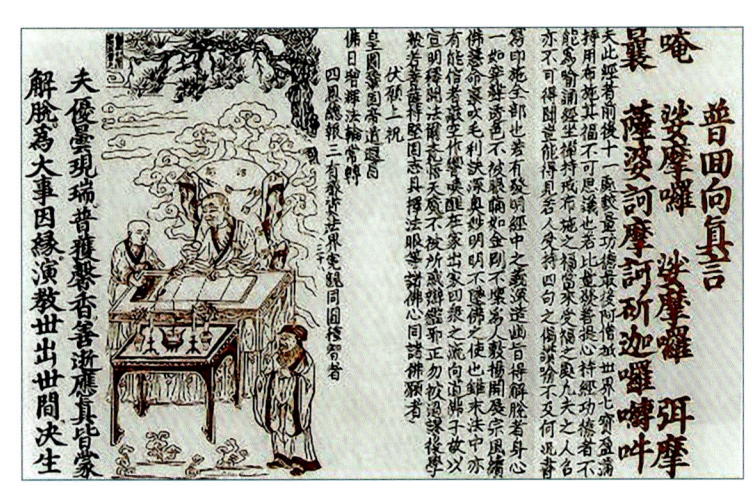

毕升开始试验。他先用木头刻了许多单字，用蜡和松香粘住这些字。这些字能拼能拆，就叫它"活字"。可是经过几次印刷之后，木活字被水泡变形了；拆字时，蜡和松香粘在木活字上怎么也洗不干净。毕升左思右想，一日，他看到小孩子玩的骰(tóu)子，是用胶泥烧的，又结实又不怕水。毕升想能不能用胶泥做"活字"呢？他试着在胶泥上刻字，做成一个个字印，再用火烧，烧成泥活字。他成功了！

泥活字好处很多，不仅刻字容易，也不变形。印书的时候，只要把"活字"按照稿件排在字盘上，用蜡固定住，压平，便可以印刷了。印完后，把活字拆下来，可以再次使用。这样印书，又快又省力，还省钱。后来，元代的王祯(zhēn)又把硬木刻成活字。他还制作了转轮

毕升泥活字版（模型）

排字架,方便排字。

活字印刷术是一个重大的发明,印书变得又快又简单。后来,印刷术传到朝鲜、日本、阿拉伯和欧洲。

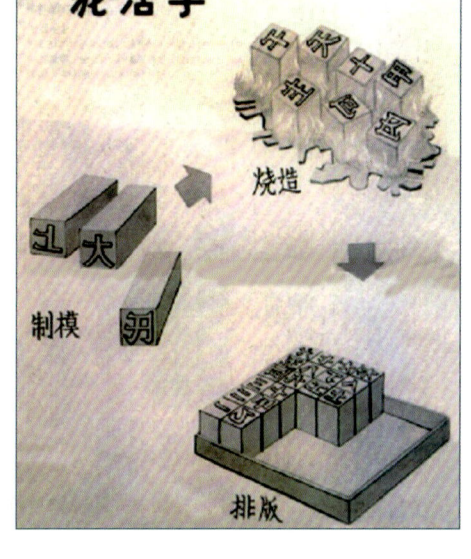

王金泰 画

生 词

yìn shuā 印刷	printing		chāi kāi 拆开	take apart
chāo xiě 抄写	copy (by handwriting)		là 蜡	wax
sù dù 速度	speed		zhān 粘	stick, glue
diāo bǎn 雕版	woodblock printing		pào 泡	soak
bì shēng 毕升	Bi Sheng; *a name*		jiāo ní 胶泥	clay
gōng jiàng 工匠	craftsman		jiē shi 结实	firm
zuò fèi 作废	go to waste		gǎo jiàn 稿件	manuscript
bǔ 补	fix, mend		yā píng 压平	press flat

听 写

抄写　速度　雕版　工匠　作废　补　拆开　粘

泡　稿件　*胶泥　压平

比一比

补 { 补衣服 / 补考 / 补课 }　　版 { 雕版 / 出版 }　　废 { 作废 / 废物 / 废纸 }

版 = 片 + 反　　粘 = 米 + 占

反义词

拼成——拆开　　泡——晾　　固定——流动

词语运用

不仅……也……

① 现在<u>不仅</u>飞机票便宜，飞机上<u>也</u>不算挤。

② 古代中国人<u>不仅</u>发明了纸，<u>也</u>发明了活字印刷术。

③ 哥哥<u>不仅</u>学习好，体育活动<u>也</u>从不落后。

作废

① 这张电影票是昨天的，已经作废了。

② 我的信用卡，明天就到期作废了。

词语解释

骰子——也叫色(shǎi)子，桌上游戏中的小道具

松香——松脂，不溶于水

左思右想——想来想去

变形——体积或形态的改变

阅读

印章、拓(tà)片与印刷术

在印刷术产生之前，印章和拓片可以说是印刷术的前身。

印章在先秦时就有，一般只有几个字，刻在铜或者石头等材料上，表示姓名、官职(zhí)或机构(gòu)。印文刻成反字，有阴文、阳文之别。也有的用于信件的"泥封"。

碑刻，是将文字刻在石碑上。汉代以后碑刻很多，古人用纸蒙在碑上拓印下来。这也是一种复制方法。有人说，拓片是历史的复印机。印章和拓片给印刷术提供了直接的经验。

阴文

阳文

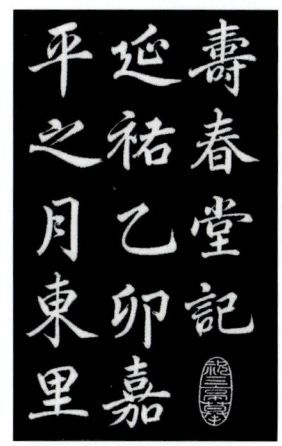
赵孟頫《寿春堂记》 碑文

王　祯

在14世纪，元朝的农学家王祯，将毕升的泥活字改成了木活字。他用坚硬的木头刻了三万多个字，并用竹片将拼好的字夹紧。这样印出来的书更清楚，质量也更好了。

王祯又制造了"转轮排字架"，由两个大轮盘组成。将常用的字放在一个轮盘中，不常用的字放在另外一个轮盘中。一个人念稿，一个人检字，又快又省力。

资料

手抄本

西汉时中国就有了纸，唐代又有了雕版印刷术，但印刷出版的书还是少数，大量的书依然用手抄写。书也被分为"抄本"和"刻本"两种。"抄本"并不便宜，所以读书求学还是很难。活字印刷术的发明，是给人类的一份礼物，使学习容易了，传播(bō)文化更简单了。现在，有了"电子书"，让人们分分钟就知道全球的信息！

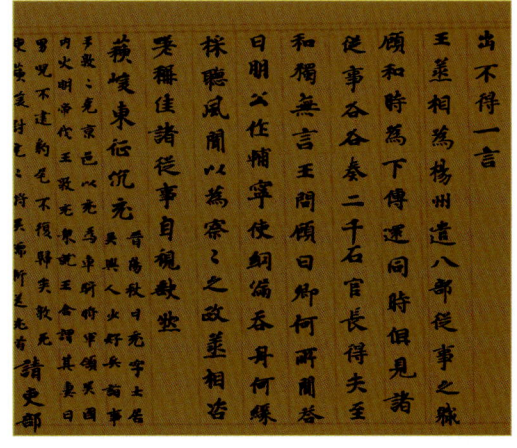

唐代手抄本

两把刷子

现在人们常用"有两把刷子"来形容人技术高，有本事。古代印刷术中，还真需要两把刷子。第一把刷子是往雕好的版上刷墨；之后，再小心地把白纸铺(pū)在版面上，用另一把干净的刷子轻轻刷纸。印刷的浓淡与凹进去的深浅有关，深了就浓，浅了就淡。所以，能用好这两把刷子，需要有很高的技术。

Lesson Four

The Four Great Inventions, Part 4
Movable Type

Before printing was invented, all books had to be copied by hand. This is very slow work.

In the middle of Tang period, the woodblock printing was invented. Each character had to be cut into a hardwood board, stroke by stroke, to produce the woodblock for printing a page. This was much faster than copying by hand. But a woodblock could be used only for printing the exact same page. If anything in the text changed, a new block had to be cut.

In the twelfth century (the Northern Song), Bi Sheng invented printing with movable types.

Bi Sheng grew up in a poor family. He studied for a few years and then went to work in a printing workshop. His work was hard; he spent each day from morning till night carving characters. But if any character turned out wrong, the whole block was wasted. Could this be helped? He found a way to fix errors: He carved out the wrong character, cut a new one and fit it into woodblock. Delighted about this success, Bi Sheng had another idea: if he used small wood cubes to cut each character separately, he could combine them in lines and take them apart again for further use. Wouldn't this make things much easier?

Bi Sheng tried it out. He cut a great many characters and stuck them together with beeswax and pine resin. He could put his types together and take them apart again, they had become movable types. But after many prints, during which the types were soaked in water, they lost their shape. Besides he found that he could not clean the wax and pine resin off completely. Bi Sheng racked his brains without finding a solution. One day he saw a child play with dice made from fired clay. Hard and water resistant: Could this be the solution for his movable types? He cut characters in clay and fired them. This time he succeeded!

Clay movable type had many advantages. They were not only easy to cut, but stable in shape. For preparing a printing block, the types could be arranged in lines as in the manuscript, fixed with wax and pressed flat. Once printing was completed, the block could be taken apart and used again. The new printing technology was not only more work-efficient, but also more economic. Some time later in the Yuan period, Wang Zhen developed movable type cut from hardwood cubes. He also invented revolving type tables that for easier made typesetting.

Movable type was a major invention in printing technologies that made the production of books faster and easier. It later spread to Korea, Japan, Arabia and Europe.

Seals, Rubbings, and Printing

Seals and rubbings from stone inscriptions can be regarded as forerunners of printing technology.

Seals can be traced back to the pre-Qin period. They usually consisted of only a few characters, such as a name, a title and an organization, and were also made from stone or bronze. The characters could be sunk into the surface or raised above it. Seals were also usually used to sign and seal letters.

Stele inscriptions were cut into slabs of stone and became common from the Han period. Stone inscriptions could be reproduced by paper rubbings, which is a printing technique. Rubbings are therefore sometimes called historic photocopies. Both seals and rubbings from stone inscriptions provided experiences directly useful for printing books.

Wang Zhen

Wang Zhen, best known for his studies of agriculture, lived in the fourteenth century (the Yan period). He changed Bi Sheng's clay movable type to wooden movable type. He used hardwood to cut over thirty thousand characters and wedged them together with bamboo splints. This improved the clarity and quality of the prints.

Wang Zhen also made a revolving table typecase. These were two revolving tables in which the frequently used characters were in one table and the rarely used ones in the other table. One person read out the manuscript, while the other picked and set the types: a quick and efficient process.

Handwritten Manuscripts

Paper was in use in China since the Western Han, and woodblock printing since the Tang period, yet only a small number of books were printed, while most written texts continued to be handwritten manuscripts. There were "handcopied" and "carved" books. "Handcopied" books were expensive and this made studying difficult. Printing with movable type was a gift to humankind, it made learning accessible and spreading writing culture easy. Nowadays, with "e-books", we can circulate news around the globe within minutes!

Wielding Two Brushes

When we admire a person for his or her skills, we say that he or she "wields two brushes". This expression actually comes from traditional printing, which required two brushes. The printer used the first brush to ink the woodblock in black ink. This done, he placed white paper on top of the block, and brushed lightly with a clean brush. The intensity of the imprint depended on the depth of the carved lines in the woodblock, rendering the lines darker where they were deeper and lighter where they were shallower. For this reason, perfect use of the two brushes indeed meant excellence for printers.

第五课

丝　绸

　　丝绸生产起源于中国，中国也被称为"丝绸之国"。早在五六千年以前，中国人就养蚕，用蚕丝织成丝绸做衣服穿。传说是黄帝的妻子嫘(léi)祖发明了养蚕。1958年，考古学家在浙江发现了4,700年前的丝线和绢片；商代的甲骨文中也有桑、蚕、丝、帛等古文字；我们在《诗经》中也读到采桑、养蚕的诗歌……可见，养蚕取丝在中国很早以前就开始了。

　　丝绸，"衣被天下"，意思是丝绸造福人类，可做衣服、被褥(rù)

"丝"字

给人们用。丝绸只能做衣服、被褥吗？当然不是，它的用途可多呢。比如作书作画，现在我们还可以看到战国时期的帛书。又比如，丝还可用来做乐器、弓箭、工资、礼品或用来交税。

丝绸的衣服又美丽，又柔软。到了汉朝，中国的丝绸纺织技术已相当发达。在长沙马王堆的汉墓中，就发现了精美的丝织品：一件素纱做成的单衣，又轻又薄，只有48克重。到了唐宋时期，丝织品已是各式各样，美丽非凡。唐代制造的一种丝绸非常薄，两面都有花纹，挂在窗户上还能透过光线。另外，还有一种用百鸟的羽毛和蚕丝织成的裙子，正看是一色，侧看是一色；白天看是一色，灯下看又是一色，十分神奇。

1934年，在长沙附近战国楚墓中，发现一件帛书，被称"楚缯书"。上面有毛笔黑墨书写的文字，四周有彩色奇异图像。全帛共一千多字。原件现藏美国耶鲁大学图书馆，是我国目前出土最早的帛书。

大约在公元前2世纪,古罗马人终于得到了丝绸——那个来自远方的神秘产品。据说,罗马的恺(kǎi)撒(sā)大帝穿着丝袍到剧院看戏,丝袍华丽无比,全场轰动。丝绸受到了罗马人的追捧,价格十分昂贵,但是昂贵的价格也挡不住时尚界的兴趣。

那么,丝绸又是怎样从遥远的中国来到罗马的呢?很早以前,就有一条商道,联系欧亚大陆。中国的丝绸就是通过这条路来到中亚和欧洲的。后来,这条路被称为"丝绸之路"。

纺织(汉画像石)

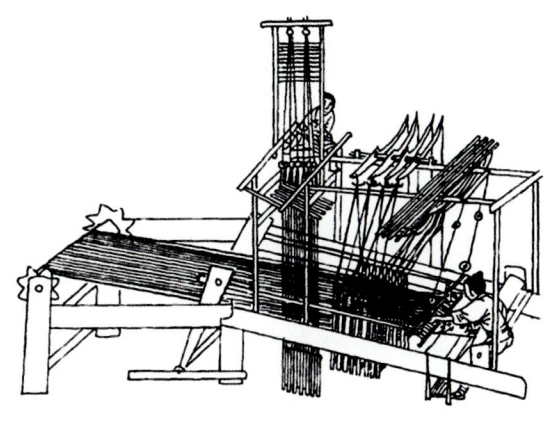

《天工开物》中的花楼机图

生词

sī chóu 丝绸	silk	huā wén 花纹	pattern
juàn 绢	plain silk	cè kàn 侧看	look at something at an angle
yòng tú 用途	use	shén mì 神秘	wonderful
gōng zī 工资	wage	chǎn pǐn 产品	product
jiāo shuì 交税	pay tax	sī páo 丝袍	silk robe
róu ruǎn 柔软	soft	hōng dòng 轰动	create a sensation
fǎng zhī 纺织	weaving	zhuī pěng 追捧	be crazy for
sù shā 素纱	raw silk gauze	jià gé 价格	price
kè 克	gram	áng guì 昂贵	elevated
gè shì gè yàng 各式各样	all kinds of	shí shàng jiè 时尚界	fashion world

听写

丝绸　用途　工资　交税　柔软　纺织　克　各式各样

花纹　神秘　产品　价格　昂贵　时尚界　*侧　追捧

比一比

途 { 用途 / 中途 / 路途 }   赏 { 欣赏 / 赏赐 }   价 { 价格 / 价钱 }

侧面      侧看

反义词

昂贵——便宜   神秘——平常

词语运用

交税

① 买汽车、买房子都要交税。

② 在飞机上买的化妆品和酒不用交税。

③ 古代中国，丝绸可以用来交税。

时尚

① 这个包很时尚。

② 老年人一般对时尚不感兴趣。

③ 姐姐的衣服总是很时尚。

词语解释

非凡——超过一般；不寻常

华丽——美丽而有光彩

各式各样——许多不同的式样

阅读

丝绸之路

汉朝初年，匈奴(xiōng nú)常常进犯汉朝国土。公元前139年，汉武帝派张骞(qiān)出使西域(yù)，联合西域各国共同攻打匈奴。

张骞走到半路，就被匈奴抓住了，并让他去放羊。十年后，他逃了出来，继续西行，来到西域的大月氏(zhī)国。大月氏的国王不想再和匈奴打仗了，但他对张骞十分热情。在那里，张骞看到了

大suàn蒜、胡luó bo萝卜等好多从来没见过的东西。回到汉朝,他把西域各国的山川、人口、风俗等情kuàng况报告给皇帝。

公元前123年,汉朝出兵打败了匈奴。从此汉朝去西域的道路开通了。中国的丝绸由长安运往中亚和欧洲。这就是著名的丝绸之路。

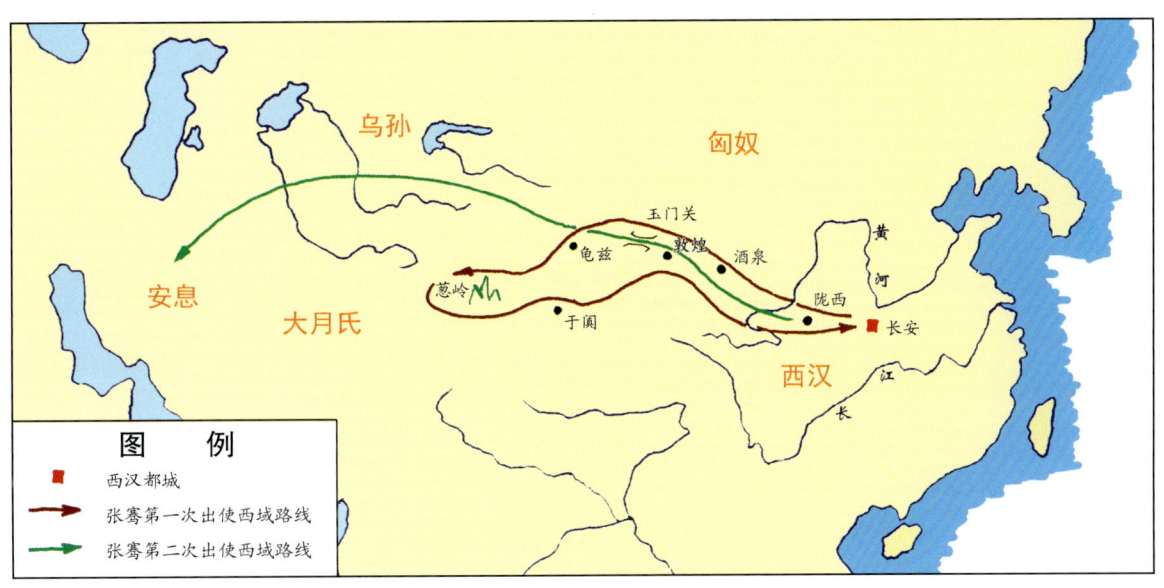

诗歌

蚕　妇

(宋)张俞yú

昨日入城市,归来泪满巾。

遍身罗绮qǐ者,不是养蚕人。

绞丝旁（jiǎo）

汉字中带绞丝旁的字，大约有200多个。其中的许多字与丝绸的生产相关。比如"缫"（sāo）丝，就是把茧子放入热水中，找出丝头抽（chōu）丝。丝很"细"，容易打"结"，"缠"（chán）死，"绞"在一起。丝"绕"好后就可以建"经"（经线），之后开始"纺""织"。丝绸织好后，剪下来（"绝"），再染（rǎn）色。这些颜色中有"红"色、"绿"色。织出的丝绸品种很多，每个品种都有自己的名字如："绢""纱""绫"（líng）"缎"（duàn）等。还有用"线""缝"衣服、"绣"（xiù）花等。一连串的字都有绞丝旁。

养蚕知识

养蚕,一年能养几次?听说过春蚕、夏蚕、秋蚕的说法吗?

中国土地辽阔,一年可以多次养蚕。

华北地区,5月至9月,一年可养蚕2~3次。

长江流域,4月下旬至10月中下旬,一年可养蚕4~5次。

珠江流域,3月至11月,一年可养蚕7~8次。

养春蚕时,气候温暖,桑叶新出,蚕不容易生病,蚕丝最好。

思考题

想一想,查一查,为什么"纸"字也是绞丝旁?

Lesson Five

Silk

Silk originated in China, which therefore has been called Serica, "the land of silk". Five- or six-thousand years ago, people in China began raising silkworms and using their silk to make clothes. According to legend, Leizu, the wife of the Yellow Emperor, invented silk. In 1958, some archaeologists discovered silk wads and silk thread made 4,700 years ago in Zhejiang. In the oracle writings on bones, we already find characters for mulberry trees, silkworms and silk cloth. *Classic of Poetry* contains poems on picking mulberry leaves and raising silkworms. Raising silkworms for their silk began very early in China.

Silk benefits people of the world by making clothes and bedding for them. Are these all the uses of silk? Of course not. There are many other uses, such as a material for calligraphy or painting—we still have texts written on silk that date back to the Warring States period, in music instruments, in bows and arrows, in wages, in gifts, and as a means of paying taxes.

Silk clothes are beautiful as well as soft. By the Han period, silk weaving technologies were advanced in China. At Mawangdui in Changsha, a grave with magnificent silks was excavated, containing a gauze robe, light and thin, weighing only 48 grams. By the Tang and Song, many beautiful types of silk were in use. A special gauze produced in the Tang period had different patterns on both sides, yet was so thin that it let the sunlight through when used as a curtain. Perhaps most amazing were silk skirts embroidered with the feathers of a hundred birds that changed their colors depending on the angle from which you looked at them and on whether you saw them in daylight or candlelight.

Roughly in the second century BC, Romans encountered silk, a product of mysterious from distant lands. There is a story that Julius Caesar caused a sensation when he wore a silk toga to the theatre. The craze for silk in Roman society drove up silk prices. Yet even great cost did not deter fashion and fascination.

But how did silk get across the vast distance from China to Rome? For a long time, a trade route linked China to Eurasia. Chinese silk reached Central Asia and Europe by this road, which is called the Silk Road.

The Silk Road

In the early Han period, the Xiongnu frequently invaded the Han empire. In 139 BC, the Emperor Wu of Han sent Zhang Qian to the Western Regions to forge an alliance against the Xiongnu.

Zhang Qian set out, but was captured by the Xiongnu halfway and made to work as a shepherd. Ten years later, he escaped and continued his westward journey. He finally reached the land of the Greater Yuezhi. Their king did not wish for another war with Xiongnu, but was very kind to Zhang Qian. In this country, Zhang Qian first learnt about the garlic, carrot and other things new to him. He returned home and reported to the emperor all that he had found out about the landscape, the people and the customs in the Western Regions.

In 123 BC, the Han armies vanquished the Xiongnu. Thus, the routes into the Western Regions were opened, and silk exports from Chang'an to Central Asia and Europe began. This trade route is the famous Silk Road.

A Silkworm-Raising Woman
by Zhang Yu (Song Period)

Yesterday I went to the market in the city;
when I returned home, my kerchief was wet with tears.
Those persons in the fine gauze and embroidered silks
are not those who raise the silkworms.

The Silk Radical

There are over 200 Chinese characters with the silk radical, and many of them have something to do with silk production. For example, 缫 means putting silkworm cocoons in hot water, looking for the end of the silk thread and winding it up. Because silk is fine, it is 细; because it's easy to tie, binding a knot is 结, strangling is 缠, and 绞 is twisted together. Once the silk thread is 绕(winding), the 经 (warp) can be set up, and then one can start 纺 and 织(weaving). When the silk cloth is woven, it is 绝 (cut into pieces) and then dyed. Dying colors are 红 (red) and 绿 (green). Finished silks come in many varieties: 绢 (plain silk), 纱 (gauze), 绫 (chiffon), 缎 (satin) and many more. And then we use 线 (yarn) to 缝 (sew) our clothes; we may even 绣 (embroider) them. All these characters are with the silk radical!

Silkworm Knowledge

How many times can silkworms be raised in a year? Have you heard of spring silkworms, summer silkworms and autumn silkworms?

China is a large country, and silkworms can be raised several times in a single year:

In North China, the season is from May to September, and two to three hatches can be raised.

In the Yangtze Valley, the season is late April to mid-to-late October, and four to five hatches can be raised.

In the Pearl River Delta, the season is March to November, and seven to eight hatches can be raised.

Spring silkworms are the best, because the weather is warm, the mulberry leaves fresh, the silkworms unlikely to get diseases, and their silk the best quality.

第六课

李春造桥

中国河北省有座古桥叫赵州桥,是一千多年前隋朝石匠李春设计的。

李春出生在河北赵州,父亲是个瓦匠。他从小跟着父亲学习技术,非常努力,还常常向老师傅请教。

李春的故乡赵州城,往南5里地有一条大河叫洨(xiáo)河。每到夏秋两季雨水很大,洨河涨水,给两岸百姓带来许多不便。人们希

赵州桥

望建造一座又牢固又方便行船的大桥。这件事在当时来说是很困难的。因为桥要牢固就要有桥墩，而有了桥墩就不方便行船。李春想了很久，他想到：建房屋常用拱形结构，建桥为什么不能用呢？他设计了一个单孔拱形石桥，桥体两边各开两个小桥洞。平时河水从大桥洞流过，发大水时河水还可以从四个小桥洞流过。这样减少了流水对桥身的冲力，桥就不容易被水冲坏，同时还减轻了桥的重量，节省了石料。

赵州桥全长50.8米，宽9.6米，而桥的高度只有7米，所以桥面平缓，无论车马还是行人过桥都不吃力。拱形还使桥身看上去十分美观，被人们比作一弯新月和雨后长虹。

一千四百多年过去了，经过了无数次的风雨、洪水和地震，这座古桥至今完好地横跨在洨河上，每天迎接着过往的车马行人。

生词

suí cháo 隋朝	Sui dynasty	jié gòu 结构	structure
shè jì 设计	design	chōng lì 冲力	impact
wǎ jiàng 瓦匠	tile maker	jié shěng 节省	save
shī fu 师傅	master craftsman	píng huǎn 平缓	mild (of a slope)
qǐng jiào 请教	ask for instructions	měi guān 美观	beautiful
zhǎng shuǐ 涨水	rising waters, high waters	wān 弯	curve
láo gù 牢固	sturdy	dì zhèn 地震	earthquake
qiáo dūn 桥墩	bridge pillar	héng kuà 横跨	lead across
gǒng xíng 拱形	arch	guò wǎng 过往	past

听写

设计　请教　涨　牢固　节省　平缓　美观　弯

地震　横跨　*瓦匠　结构

比一比

{ 拱（拱形）
  洪（洪水） }

{ 弯（弯曲）
  湾（台湾） }

{ 缓（平缓）
  暖（温暖） }

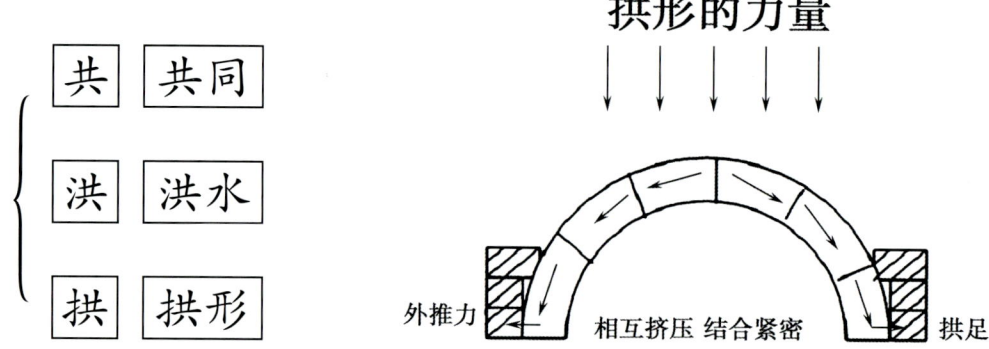

"牢"字的演化

牢固——坚固结实　　牢：牛马圈

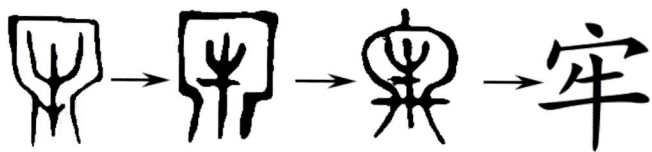

词语运用

设计

① 李春设计和建造了赵州桥。

② 姐姐在大学里学习服装设计。

③ 爸爸是工程师，他是设计飞机发动机的。

平缓

① 上山的路很平缓，我们爬到山顶并不吃力。

② 赵州桥桥面平缓，无论马车还是行人过桥都不吃力。

至今

① 去年妈妈就说给我买一条新裙子，可她至今还没给我买。

② 中国古代发明的传统造纸方法，至今仍然被使用。

阅读

古桥的故事

天下有山谷，有河流，自然就有了"桥"。它们有的是倒下的一棵树，有的是一些石头块。

一、梁桥。中国最早出现的桥是梁桥。梁桥外形平直，有桥墩。中国现存最早的梁桥，是西安灞河上的"灞(bà)桥"，它始建于2,000多年前的春秋时期。

灞桥

二、拱桥。拱桥是桥梁建筑的一朵奇花。它不但构造先进、坚固，而且造型(xíng)千变万化，很是美观，如大家知道的赵州桥。

三、浮桥和梁桥结合。广东潮州，有一座著名的古桥——广济桥。广济桥建于公元1171年（宋朝）。桥的结构(shū)十分特殊，是浮桥和梁桥的结合。桥的两边是梁桥，桥中间由浮桥相连，桥面是古色古香的亭阁(tíng gé)。每日定时收起浮桥，让货船通过，所以桥又牢固，又方便行船。

广济桥

广济桥中段浮桥

资料

- 港珠澳大桥是桥隧(suì)结合的跨海大桥，全长55千米，包括一条长6.7千米的海底隧道及两个人工岛。

- 北盘江大桥位于贵州，是世界第一高桥。大桥长1,341.4米，高565米，相当于一座200层高的摩(mó)天大楼。贵州是个多山的地方，现在，全省已有21,000多座桥梁，交通比以前方便了很多。

- 云天渡(dù)玻(bō)璃(li)桥全长430米，是世界上最长的玻璃桥。它建在山美水美的湖南张家界。

港珠澳大桥

北盘江大桥

云天渡玻璃桥

Lesson Six

Li Chun, the Bridge Builder

The Zhaozhou Bridge is an ancient bridge in Hebei Province in China that was designed by Master Mason Li Chun more than a thousand years ago in the Sui period.

Li Chun was born in Zhao County, Hebei Province, and his father was a tile-maker. From childhood, Li Chun learnt construction technologies from his father, always working hard and often asking old masters for instructions.

Li Chun's hometown was Zhao County, and five *li* south of the city was a large river called Xiaohe River. Each summer to autumn during the rainy period, the river swelled. People along the river faced many difficulties. If only there was a bridge that was solid yet let the boats through! At the time such a structure seemed impossible. A solid bridge had to have thick pillars, and thick pillars would be in the way of the boats. Li Chun racked his brains for a long time, until he had an idea: Arches were used in buildings, why not in bridges? He designed a single-arch bridge with two smaller arches near each bank. Thus the river would flow through the middle arch at ordinary water levels, and had the extra room of the four smaller arches during high water levels. This reduced the impact of the flow on the bridge and hence the danger of the bridge being damaged over time. At the same time, it reduced the weight of the bridge and thus saved materials.

The Zhaozhou Bridge is 50.8 meters long and 9.6 meters wide, but only 7 meters high. Although an arch bridge, it is not steep, and horse carts as well as pedestrians cross it without effort. Moreover, the arch is elegant and has been compared to a new moon or a rainbow.

One-thousand and four-hundred years have passed, with rainstorms, floods, and earthquakes, yet the ancient bridge stands firm, each day providing people and carts with the means to cross the Xiaohe River.

About Ancient Bridges

Natural bridges exist because there are valleys, rivers and streams in the world, and a tree or a stone slab might fall across a watercourse.

In China, the earliest bridges were beam bridges. They consist of pillars and straight beams. The oldest extant beam bridge is the Ba Bridge in Xi'an. It was built over 2,000 years ago in the Spring and Autumn period.

Arch bridges are the most elegant of all bridges. Their structure is more advanced and robust than beam bridges and they come in many beautiful shapes, such as the well-known Zhaozhou Bridge.

Composite pontoon-beam bridges. The Guangji Bridge in Chaozhou, Guangdong Province, is a famous historic bridge built in 1171 during the Song period. Its structure is special: It is partly a beam bridge, but with a pontoon section in the middle. The permanent bridge carries pavilions in ancient style, and everyday at a certain time, the pontoon section is opened to allow to freight boats to pass through. This structure is at once solid and convenient for the passage of boats.

Materials

The Hong Kong-Zhuhai-Macau Bridge (HZMB) is a 55-kilometer bridge-tunnel system, which is also a cross-sea bridge. It consists of a 6.7-kilometer undersea tunnel and 2 artificial islands.

The Beipan River Bridge, located in Guizhou, is the tallest bridge in the world. The bridge is 1,314.4 meters long and 565 meters high, which is equivalent to a 200-storey skyscraper. Guizhou is a mountainous place, now there are more than 21,000 bridges, and the traffic is much more convenient than before.

Yuntiandu Glass Bridge is the longest glass bridge in the world with a total length of 430 meters. It was built in Zhangjiajie, Hunan Province, which is a place with beautiful mountains and waters.

第七课

扁鹊的四诊法

春秋战国时期，有位名医叫扁鹊，他是中医的奠基人之一。中医诊病的基本方法"四诊法"：望、闻、问、切，是扁鹊最早系统使用的。

扁鹊，本名秦越人。那时人们重鬼神而轻医术。一旦有瘟疫流行，国家就请巫师来驱鬼。秦越人年轻时在一家客店干活儿。一年瘟疫流行，巫师们驱鬼已十几天了，可死的人却越来越多。秦越人见到巫术害人，也见到一位叫长桑君的老医生四处治病救人，便拜老医生为师开始学医。他上山采药，学习医术。几年后他精通了针灸、手术、汤药等各种医术，成为远近闻名的医生。

一次晋国大夫赵简(jìn)子病危，昏睡了五天，粒米未进，秦越人将他治好；又一次他将已死半日的虢(guó)国太子救活；他还救助了无数病人，于是人们送他一个美名——神医扁鹊。扁鹊是传说中的

扁鹊与蔡桓公

神鸟,它会用长长的嘴给人治病。从此,秦越人的名字却渐渐被人忘了。

当时中国分成许多小国,扁鹊带着弟子在各地行医。一次他见到蔡桓(huán)公,便说蔡桓公有病,病在皮肤下,应马上治疗才好。蔡桓公不信,认为医生都喜欢把好人说成病人,以显示自己的本领。过了几天,扁鹊再见到蔡桓公时,又说:"您的病到了血脉,再不治会加重的。"蔡桓公还是不信,让扁鹊走了。又过了几天,扁鹊去见蔡桓公,说:"您的病到了肠胃,再不治就危险了。"蔡桓公还是不听。又过了几天,扁鹊再次见到蔡桓公时,什么话也没说,转身就走。别人问他为什么走,他说,病到了骨髓,已无药可治了。不久蔡桓公果然发病死了。

弟子问扁鹊,怎能隔着肚皮看清病人的内脏?扁鹊说:"我看病主要靠四诊法——望、闻、问、切。望:看病人脸色、舌头;闻:听病人发出的声音,嗅(xiù)病人身上的气味;问:问病人的情况和病史;切:触摸病人身体和把脉。这四种诊断法,使我诊断准确。"

扁鹊到八十岁时,还出游行医。当他来到秦国时,秦太医怕秦王重用扁鹊,便派人杀害了扁鹊。扁鹊的医疗理论和经验由弟子们传下来,并在汉朝时被写成一部医书《黄帝八十一难经》,这本书对医学发展有很大的影响。

洪涛　冯聪英　画

生词

biǎn què 扁鹊	Bian Que, a name	zhì liáo 治疗	cure, heal
zhěn 诊	cure, treat an illness	xuè mài 血脉	blood vessel
diàn jī 奠基	lay the foundation	cháng wèi 肠胃	stomach and intestines
yí dàn 一旦	as soon as	gǔ suǐ 骨髓	bone marrow
wēn yì 瘟疫	infectious disease	chù mō 触摸	touch
liú xíng 流行	spread around	yī liáo 医疗	medical treatment
qū guǐ 驱鬼	exorcise, drive out noxious spirits	lǐ lùn 理论	theory
zhēn jiǔ 针灸	acupuncture	jīng yàn 经验	experience
tāng yào 汤药	decoction		

听写

扁鹊　诊　一旦　瘟疫　流行　针灸　治疗　肠胃

医疗　理论　经验　*奠基　血脉

比一比

脉 { 山脉 / 把脉 / 血脉 }　　疗 { 治疗 / 医疗 }　　诊 { 门诊 / 诊断 }

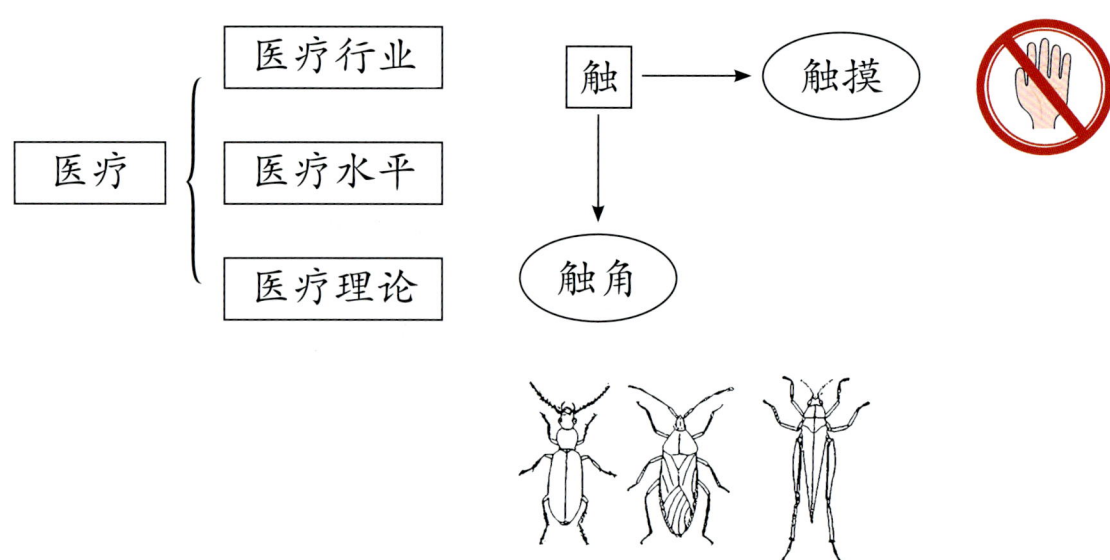

同音字

wēn	wēn
温	瘟
温度	瘟疫

词语运用

诊断

① 医生诊断爷爷是得了胃病。

② 妈妈的病，两位医生的诊断是相同的。

③ 没有医生的诊断，你怎么能乱吃药！

经验

① 这位老医生很有经验。

② 我会开车，但是没有开大客车的经验。

③ 这位新老师教学经验还不够。

一旦

① 他一旦病好了，还会去爬山。

② 哥哥一旦有钱了，就会去买一辆新车。

③ 一旦停电了，我们连热水都喝不上。

词语解释

手术——外科手术简称手术,俗称开刀

病史——本人或家族患病的历史

阅读

起死回生

一次扁鹊到了虢国,在街上见到人们仨(sā)一群俩(liǎ)一伙地说:"太子刚刚死了。"于是扁鹊赶到王宫,见到床上的太子,脸色苍白,牙关紧咬。扁鹊给太子摸脉,感到虽然他身体冰凉,但还有微脉在跳。扁鹊断定太子还没有死,马上取针急救。不久太子果然醒了过来。之后,扁鹊又用汤药给太子调理,二十多天过去了,太子的病全好了。这件事传出后,人们都说扁鹊有起死回生的本领。

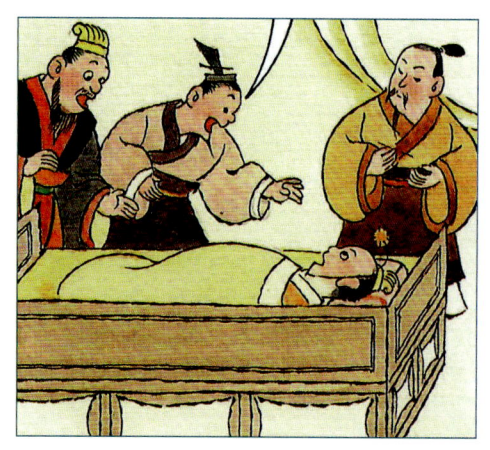

洪涛　冯聪英　画

王惟一(wéi)

王惟一（约987—1067），宋代医学家，中国第一个设计和铸造了"针灸教学人体模(mó)型"的人。

针灸疗法在中国有至少有2,500年的历史。早在公元630年，唐朝名医孙思邈(miǎo)就绘(huì)制了彩色针灸挂图。唐朝以后，针灸疗法作为独立的一科，被正式列入官方医学教育课程。王惟一为了针灸教学，向皇帝提出制造铜人模型。公元1027年，两个铜人模型铸造出来。铜人全身有354个穴(xué)位名称，657个针灸点。有机关可以打开模型的前胸，看到铜人的五脏。

王惟一总结了以前针灸学的经验，改正了许多不正确的穴位数据(jù)，写成了三卷《铜人腧(shù)穴针灸图经》。

针灸铜人
造件铜人是明人依宋制仿造的。铜人全身共有666个针灸点，既是针灸医疗的范本，又是医官院教学和考试的工具。

资料

扁 鹊

扁鹊,姬(jī)姓,秦氏,名越人,春秋战国时期名医。他少年时跟从长桑君学医,到各国行医,精通各科。因医术高明,老百姓便借用神话中的神医"扁鹊"的名字来称呼他。后为秦王治病时,秦太医嫉妒他,派人把他杀害了。扁鹊的四诊法奠定了中医学的切脉诊断方法。相传中医书《黄帝八十一难经》为扁鹊所著。

河北内丘扁鹊祠

人首鸟身扁鹊鸟行医图(汉画像石)

Lesson Seven

Bian Que's Four Diagnostic Methods

Bian Que, a famous doctor and one of the founding fathers of Chinese traditional medicine, lived in the Spring and Autumn and Warring States periods. He was the first to systematically use the four-step diagnoses of "Looking, Listening, Inquiring, and Taking".

Bian Que's original name was Qin Yueren. In his time, people believed in ghosts and spirits rather than in medicine. When infectious diseases spread, governments asked wizards to drive out the noxious spirits. When Qin Yueren was young, he worked in an inn. One year, seasonal diseases were particularly bad, and wizards had been performing their exorcisms for weeks, yet more and more people died. Qin Yueren realized that witchcraft was harmful. When meeting an old doctor named Master Changsang, who treated the sick and saved many lives, he became his pupil and began studying medicine. He climbed mountains to pick medicinal herbs and studied the art of healing. A few years later, he had mastered acupuncture, operations, and decoction and became a renowned doctor.

Once, Zhao Jianzi, a minister of the State of Jin, fell gravely ill and lay unconscious for five days, unable to swallow a single grain, but Qin Yueren was able to cure him. Some time later, the Prince of the State of Guo lay dead for half a day, yet Qin Yueren brought him back to life. He saved countless lives, and people gave him the name "godlike doctor Bian Que" out of gratitude. Bian Que is a legendary magical bird that uses its long beak to treat illnesses. Hence, Qin Yueren's original name was gradually forgotten.

At the time, China consisted of many small countries, and Bian Que and his pupils traveled around all of them to practice their medicine. He once saw Cai Huangong and immediately warned him that an illness had befallen him under his skin that required immediate treatment. Cai Huangong did not believe him, thinking that doctors like to tell you that you are ill so that they can show off. A few days later, Bian Que saw Cai Huangong again and warned him that the illness had reached his veins and would become grave unless treated. Cai Huangong still did not believe him and sent him away. A few days later, Bian Que came to see Cai Huangong and told him that the illness had reached his digestive organs and that he was in danger unless he let it be treated. Cai Huangong still did not believe him. Again a few days later, Bian Que saw Cai Huangong. This time, without a single word, Bian Que turned and left. When asked about his reaction, Bian Que said that the illness had reached the marrow of Cai Huangong's bones and he was beyond cure. Shortly afterwards, Cai Huangong in fact fell ill and died.

Bian Que's pupils asked him how he could see that the illness had reached the inner organs? Bian Que explained that he used four diagnostic methods: Looking, Listening, Inquiring, and Taking. Looking meant looking at the outside appearances and the tongue of the patient; Listening meant listening to his voice and smelling his body odours; Inquiring meant asking the patient about his symptoms and former illnesses; Taking meant taking the patient's pulse. "With these four methods, I can diagnose without fail."

When Bian Que reached the age of eighty, he was still traveling around to practice medicine. When he came to the State of Qin, the court doctor of Qin feared that the King of Qin would value Bian Que's art above his own, and had him murdered. His pupils transmitted Bian Que's medical theory and experience and his medical knowledge was written down in the Han period as *The Yellow Emperor's Canon of 81 Difficult Issues*, a great contribution to the development of medicine.

Returning to Life from Death

Once upon a time, Bian Que came to the State of Guo, and on the streets encountered small groups of people who told him that the prince had just died. Bian Que rushed to the palace and saw the prince lying on his bed, white as death and his jaw tightly clenched. Bian Que felt the prince's pulse, and even though the body was cold, he still discerned a weak pulse. He concluded that the prince had not yet died and took out his needles to treat him. And behold, the prince in fact soon woke up! Later, Bian Que brewed medicines for him and after some twenty days, the prince completely recovered. Because of this feat people believed that Bian Que could bring back the dead.

Wang Weiyi

Wang Weiyi (about 987–1067) was a doctor during the Song period. He made the first human model for teaching acupuncture.

Acupuncture is a Chinese medical method that goes back 2,500 years. As early as 630 AD, the Tang doctor Sun Simiao painted a colorful picture of the acupuncture meridians. From the Tang, acupuncture became an independent discipline taught in the official medical schools. Wang Weiyi presented his bronze figure for teaching acupuncture to the emperor. By 1027 he had made two such figures. The bronze figure shows 354 names of acupuncture points (holes connected to the meridians) and 657 further points. A mechanism permits opening the chest to look at the figurine's inner organs.

Wang Weiyi comprehensively studied preceding experience in acupuncture, corrected many mistakes in the data on acupuncture points, and wrote the *Illustrated Manual* of *Acupuncture Points on a Bronze Figure*, a work in three chapters.

Bian Que

Bian Que, family name Ji, clan name Qin, given name Yueren, a famous doctor of the Spring and Autumn and Warring States periods. In his youth, Bian Que studied medicine with Master Changsang, and traveled through the countries practicing and mastering all medical disciplines. His medical art was such that is appeared magical, and the people gave him the name Bian Que, inspired by the legendary magical bird of healing. In the end, when he treated the King of Qin, the court doctor became jealous of him and had him murdered. The four-step diagnoses summarized by Bian Que laid the foundation for the development of the pulse diagnosis in Chinese medicine. According to tradition, he authored the book *The Yellow Emperor's Classic of 81 Difficult Issues*.

第八课

李时珍和他的《本草纲目》

李时珍

李时珍（1518—1593）是明代著名的医药学家。

李时珍出生在湖北一个医生家庭，从小就喜爱医学，24岁当了医生。他看病认真，关心病人。许多穷人没有钱，他也给他们看病，后来名声越来越大。

李时珍行医的时候读了许多医药书籍，发现书中有不少错误和漏写之处，而药书的错误是会害死人的。一次，李时珍见一男子大哭，说是医生把他娘治死了，要去告官。李时珍看了药方，并没有错。于是他又去检查药渣，发现是药铺抓错了一种药。他到药铺追问，药铺老板拿出药书说："书上明明写着，两种药名是同一种药。"这种事，不怪医生，不怪药铺，是药书的错误。李时珍想要写一本新的药书。父亲却说:"修'本草'是朝廷大事,你一个民间医生怎能完成?"

后来,李时珍有机会到皇宫当了医官。在那里,他阅读了大量医学典籍,眼界大开。父亲死后,他回到家乡。他想:朝廷不修"本草",我自己修!他决心写一部完善的药书。

李时珍来到民间,四方的乡民、药农、渔民听说他要重修"本草",都争相献出家传药方和药材,让李时珍非常感动。回家后,他把药方、药材对照药书一一校订整理。公元1565年,李时珍又带着古药典中数不清的疑问,开始了长达十年的旅行考察。他走访了长江、黄河流域和广东、广西等地,看到不知道名称的植物就向当地老百姓请教,弄明白特性和用途,画好图记录下来。

李时珍行万里路,收集了大量实物资料回到家中,开始编书。李时珍把药物按金石、草、兽等分类编写,很接近现代科学分类。他把每种药物的名称、产地、形态、气

《本草纲目》插图

味、治什么病及制作方法,都写在书里并附上图画。经过27年的努力,他订正了古药书中的错漏,终于写成了药物学巨著《本草纲目》。这时他已是61岁的老人了。

1596年,《本草纲目》出版,全书52卷,190万字,收入1,892种药物,插图1,109幅,药方11,096个。《本草纲目》是中国古代最完备的药书。后来,《本草纲目》被翻译成多种文字,流传于世界。

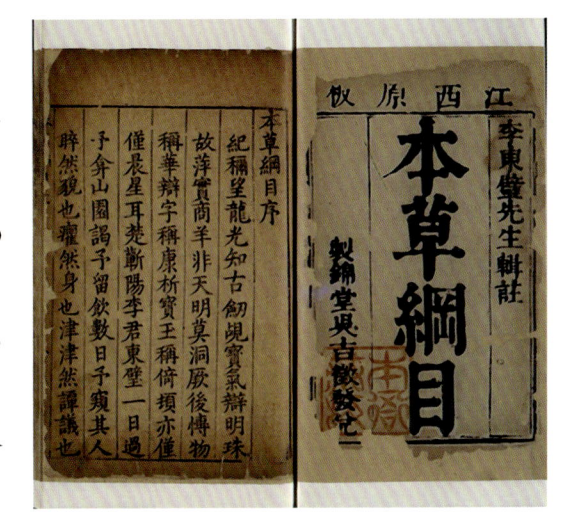

词汇接龙游戏(与"药"字有关的词汇)

药方——药房——药铺——吃药——汤药——拿药——取药

药渣——中药——西药——新药——过期药——买药——卖药

……

生词

gāng mù 纲目	compendium, systematically organized work	diǎn jí 典籍	classic works
		jiào dìng 校订	compare and correct
jiā tíng 家庭	family	yí wèn 疑问	doubt
cuò wù 错误	error	shōu jí 收集	collect
lòu xiě 漏写	left out, omit	kē xué 科学	science
yào fāng 药方	prescription	xíng tài 形态	form
yào zhā 药渣	dreg of a decoction	zhì zuò 制作	make
yào pù 药铺	drugstore	fù shang 附上	add, attach
cháo tíng 朝廷	court	juàn 卷	chapter, volume
yuè dú 阅读	read	fān yì 翻译	translate

听写

本草纲目　家庭　错误　药铺　阅读　疑问　收集　科学

形态　制作　附上　卷　*典籍　校订　翻译

比一比

典 { 典礼 / 典籍 }　　制 { 制作 / 制造 }　　修 { 修书 / 修车 / 修理 }

书籍	典籍
书的总称	古代重要文献的总称

　　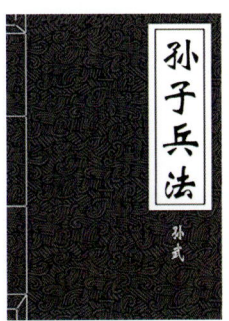

反义词

科学——迷信　　错误——正确　　疑问——确信/相信

多音字

xiào	jiào
校	校
学校	校订

词语运用

错误

① 小弟弟总犯错误，这不，又把花踩断了。

② 李时珍发现古药书中有许多错误。

③ 人都会犯错误，知道错，改了就好。

阅读

① 我们学习中文，每周都有阅读课。

② 要有阅读习惯，成为终生热爱学习的人。

③ 有的国家平均每人每年阅读68本书。

记录

① 录音机记录了我们的声音。

② 照相机记录了我们的身影。

③ 甲骨文记录了3,000多年前商代人的活动。

词语解释

完善——完美的

药材——在中国一般指制造中药的原料

完备——应该有的全都有了

特性——某事物所特有的性质

阅读

屠呦呦(yōu hāo)与青蒿素

屠呦呦是中国药学家，她多年从事中药和中西药结合研究。1972年，她发现一种治疗疟(nüè)疾的药物——青蒿素，救助了全球百万人的生命。2015年，屠呦呦获得诺贝尔医学奖。

疟疾是一种流行病，主要在热带和亚热带由蚊子传播。2015年，全球有2亿多人感染疟疾，43万人死亡，其中90%在非洲。屠呦呦在研究治疟疾药物时，会从中国古代医药书籍中寻求帮助。东晋葛洪的医书《肘(zhǒu)后备急方》中，对青蒿治疟疾有这样一段话："青蒿一握，以水二

屠呦呦

升渍,绞取汁,尽服之。"这段话提醒了屠呦呦,用低温提取青蒿素,终于成功了。屠呦呦说青蒿素的发现,是中国传统医学献给人类的一份礼物。

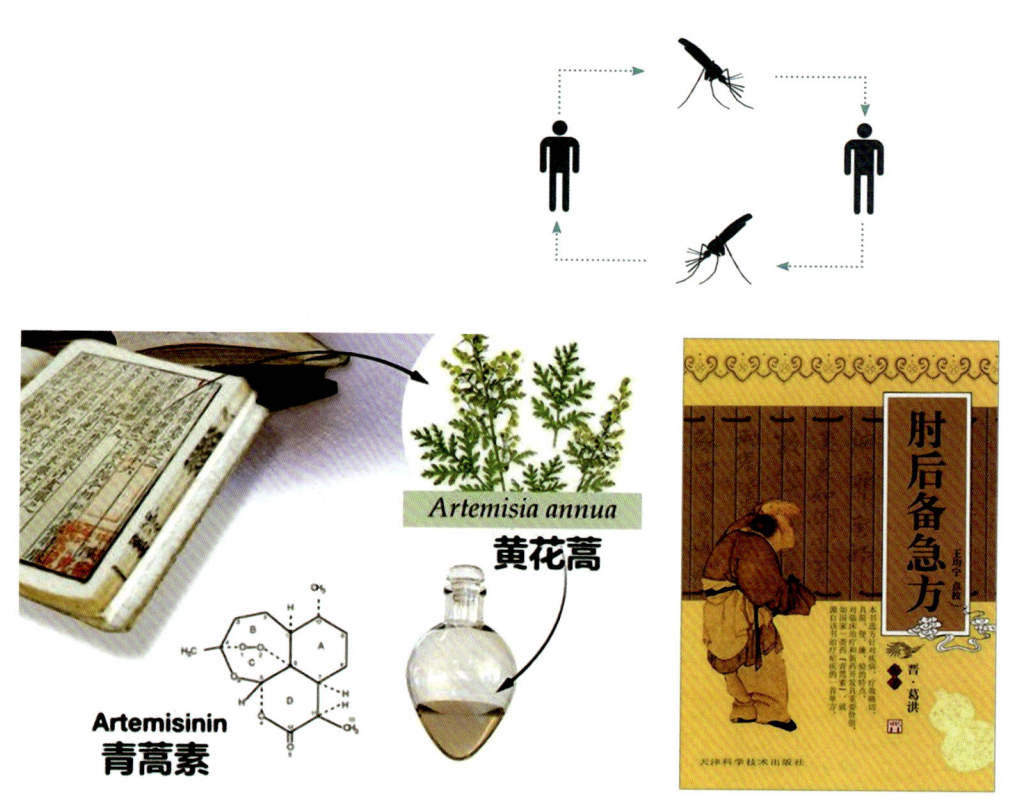

生活中常用的"中药"

中药离我们的生活很近。

在中国，人们都知道，如果风寒感冒，煮点儿"生姜红糖水"喝下去，盖上被子出一身汗，睡一觉，感冒就好了。其实，生姜、红糖、大蒜、葱白都是我们生活中常用的中药。

菊花，很常见，你可能没想到吧，喝碗菊花茶，能够达到清火去病的作用。

蜂蜜，也入药。老年人大便不通，喝点儿蜂蜜水会有帮助。

红枣，是我们喜欢吃的药食两用食材。

绿豆汤，可以清热、解毒、利尿。

茶，就更不用说了。最初，茶是药用的，帮助消化、解毒。

广东人最爱煲汤，常常把一些药材和鸡肉、猪肉放在一起煲汤。味道好又养人。

其实，许多"中药"就是我们的食材，中国人的生活是离不开这些"中药"的。

Lesson Eight

Li Shizhen and his *Compendium of Materia Medica*

Li Shizhen (1518–1593) was a famous doctor of the Ming period.

He was born into a family of doctors in Hubei and discovered his love for medicine when he was young, becoming a practicing doctor when he was only 24. He greatly cared for his patients. Many poor people could not pay him, yet he treated them just as carefully, and became more and more widely known.

He read many medical books and realized that existing works contained numerous errors and omissions. But errors in medical books can kill people! One day, Li Shizhen met a man in tears, who told him that the doctor had killed his mother by his treatment and he was going to take the doctor to court. Li Shizhen looked at the prescription, and it looked correct. He then investigated the dreg of the decoction, and found that one of the ingredients was wrong. So he went to the drugstore to find out what had happened. The druggist took out his pharmaceutical book and showed him that two substances were listed as exchangeable. The woman's death was the fault of neither the doctor, nor the druggist, but of a mistake in the book. Li Shizhen concluded that he needed to write a new book. But his father said: "Writing a systematic work on materia medica is a matter of highest importance, a matter for the imperial court. How would you, a simple doctor without any official degree be capable of such a task?"

Later on, Li Shizhen had the opportunity to become a court doctor. At the imperial court, he read many books on medicine and greatly broadened his outlook. Then his father died, and he returned home. Back home, he thought: The court is making no move to compile a new compendium, so I will!

Having taken his decision, he went out among the people to learn more. Villagers, herb growers and fishers heard about Li Shizhen and his plan, and they all came to tell him the medical substances they knew and their family drugs. Li Shizhen was deeply touched. He took all the information back home and compared it to the medical substances in the book, revising them entry by entry. As he had his doubts about the information in the medical books, in 1565, he left home to collect more information and specimens. For ten years he traveled, collecting medical substances along the Yangtze River and the Yellow River, in Guangdong, Guangxi and other regions. Whenever he found a herb that he did not know, he asked the locals. Once he understood its characteristics and uses, he made a drawing and recorded the herb.

Li Shizhen traveled ten-thousand *li*, found a great many specimens, and took them home to compile his book. He organized the medical substances under the headings minerals, herbs, and animal products etc, much like a modern scientific classification. For each substance, he recorded the name, the area where it occurred, the form and taste, and its medical purposes and manufacture methods,

adding a drawing for each entry. After 27 years of work, his great medical work, the *Compendium of Materia Medica* that corrected the errors and filled in many omissions in the older works. By this time, he was an old man of 61 years.

The book was printed in 1596, in 52 chapters and comprising 1.9 million characters. It describes 1,892 medical substances and contains 1,109 illustrations and 11,096 drug prescriptions. It is the most complete work on medical substances in pre-modern China. Later on, it has been translated into several languages and circulated worldwide.

Tu Youyou and Artemisinin

Tu Youyou is a Chinese pharmacologist who spent many years researching Chinese medicine and the combination of Chinese and Western medicine. In 1972, she discovered artemisinin, a drug against malaria, and so saved the lives of millions of people around the globe. In 2015, she received the Nobel Prize for her work.

Malaria is spread by mosquitoes in the tropics and sub-tropics. As late as 2015, over 200 million people still suffered from this disease, and 430,000 died from it, with 90% of the cases in Africa. When Tu Youyou searched for new drugs against malaria, she found guidance in ancient Chinese books on medical substances. In a book by Ge Hong of the Eastern Jin entitled *Handbook of Prescriptions of Emergency Treatments*, she read the following prescription against malaria: "Take a handful of Artemisia, soak in two liters of water, mix and drain, drink it all." Tu Youyou realized that low temperatures were important in isolating the medical substance in the artemisia plant, and at length she succeeded in isolating artemisinin. She says that the discovery of artemisinin is a gift of ancient Chinese medicine to humankind.

Everyday Uses of Chinese Medicine

Chinese medicine is part of our everyday life.

In China, it is common knowledge that when you get a cold due to cold winds, you boil some raw ginger with some cane sugar, get under thick bedcovers to work up a sweat, and go to sleep. When you wake up again, the cold is gone. Ginger, the cane sugar, garlic and scallion stalks are Chinese medicines that we frequently use.

The chrysanthemum is a common flower. Who would have thought that you can have a cup of chrysanthemum tea to reduce the internal heat of our bodies?

Honey is also part of many medicines. When an elderly person feels constipated, drinking a bit of honey might help.

Dates are a kind of really tasty medicinal fruit.

Green mung-bean soup reduces heat, cleanses the body, and promotes diuresis.

Tea hardly needs mentioning. At first, it was just used for its medical purpose, to help to digest and cleanse the body.

Cantonese are fond of slowly stewed soups, which often contain some drug ingredients, and chicken or pork, tasty and nourishing.

Many foods that we eat also have medical uses in Chinese medicine, hence Chinese medicine is always part of life.

第九课

都江堰

都江堰全景

在中国四川省成都市附近，有一个闻名世界的无坝水利工程，叫都江堰。它是战国时期李冰修建的。论年岁，它和长城一样古老，可是两千年后的今天，长城早已成为古迹，而都江堰却像个"年轻人"不分昼夜地工作，灌溉着成都平原的几百万亩良田。

都江堰建成以前，岷江时常发洪水，人民生活很苦。后来，李冰到成都做官，开始在岷江治水。他看地形了解水情，找出了水灾的原因。原来，岷江发源于岷山，每年春天，山上的雪化了，水从四面八方流入岷江。到了平原，岷江河道变窄，就会引发洪水。于是李冰想出了治水的方法。

一、宝瓶口。李冰决定在岷江刚进入平原的地方，把江水一分为二，一股水沿老河道（外江）流走；另一股水，通过新河道（内江）流入成都平原灌溉田地。这实在是个好办法。但是要开一条新河道，旁边的玉垒山挡住了去成都的路，李冰决定把山劈开。玉垒山山石坚硬，李冰让人用柴草把石头烧热，再泼上冷水，石头就裂开了。经过多年的努力，人们终于把玉垒山凿开了一个20米宽的大口子，人们叫它宝瓶口。

都江堰

二、鱼嘴。新河道开好了，为了让更多的水流入宝瓶口，李冰决定在岷江中心建一道分水堤，也叫鱼嘴。开始他们用石头建分水堤，可是洪水一来，堤就被冲垮了。李冰又想了个办法，让人编了好多大竹笼，里面装满鹅卵石，再把竹笼一排排地沉到江里去。这样，尽管水流急，却冲不走大竹笼，一道牢固的分水堤建成了。鱼嘴还利用了弯道流体力学的原理，使表层水流进内江，而含沙多的底层水流向外江，于是大部分沙石就留在外江河道里。

三、飞沙堰。飞沙堰是内江上一个不高的水堤，当洪水季节内江水量太大，宝瓶口流不过去的时候，多余的江水会越过飞沙堰又流回岷江，使成都平原可以安全灌溉。另外飞沙堰还有二次排沙的作用。

都江堰建成后，岷江再也没有水灾。成都平原变成"水旱从人，不知饥馑(jǐn)，时无荒年"的"天府之国"。后来，人们在都江堰建了一座庙纪念李冰。

都江堰示意图

生词

dū jiāng yàn 都江堰	Dujiangyan; *an irrigation system*	gǔ 股	stream
bà 坝	dam	lěi 垒	pile of stones
shuǐ lì gōng chéng 水利工程	hydro technology, irrigation works	pī kāi 劈开	cut through (*hard material*)
		jiān yìng 坚硬	hard
zhòu yè 昼夜	day and night	píng 瓶	bottle
guàn gài 灌溉	irrigate	chōng kuǎ 冲垮	be destroyed by a water current
mǔ 亩	mu; *unit of land area*	lóng 笼	cage
mín jiāng 岷江	Min River	huāng nián 荒年	famine year
zhǎi 窄	narrow		

听写

都江堰　坝　水利工程　昼夜　灌溉　亩　岷江　窄

股　瓶　冲垮　*坚硬　笼

比一比

股 { 一股 / 股票 / 屁股 }　　堤 { 河堤 / 海堤 / 分水堤 }　　水 { 水利 / 水害 / 水灾 }

反义词

宽——窄　　涨——落　　硬——软

多音字

都(dū)　　　　　　　　　　都(dōu)

都(dū) { 成都 / 都江堰 }　　都(dōu) { 都是 / 都行 }

量 词

"股",计量条状物,计量气体、气味、力气等。

一(股)泉水　　一(股)冷风　　一(股)劲头

一(股)线　　　一(股)烟味　　一(股)力量

词语运用

尽管……却……

① 尽管河水流得很急,竹笼却冲不走。

② 尽管春天到了,天气却还很冷。

③ 尽管她迟到了,老师却没说她。

阅读

神奇的都江堰

都江堰水利工程，主要由鱼嘴、飞沙堰和宝瓶口三部分组成。鱼嘴是个分水堤，把岷江分成外江和内江。外江是原来的老河道；内江是新河道，用于引水灌溉。水少季节，岷江水60%会流入内江灌溉田地；洪水季节，60%的水顺着外江河道流走。鱼嘴还利用了弯道流体力学的原理，使表层水流进内江，而含沙量多的底层水流向外江，大部分沙石就留在外江河道。飞沙堰是内江上一个不高的水堤，它高出内江河床2.15米。当内江水量超过宝瓶口流量时，多余的水便从飞沙堰流出，如有特大洪水时，它会自行溃(kuì)堤，让江水流回岷江。宝瓶口在玉垒山上，是内江流入成都平原的入水口。

宝瓶口

洪水季节，由于飞沙堰的调节，宝瓶口的入水不会过量，成都平原可以安全灌溉。

李冰父子塑像

资料

都江堰的岁修

都江堰从建成到今天，两千多年来没有损毁(huǐ)，是因为一直维修。宋朝时，订立了每年冬春（枯水时期）的岁修制度。维修时要"深淘(táo)滩，低作堰"。深淘滩中的"滩"，指的是内江和外江河道。每年洪水过后，会有许多沙石留在河床上，必须清理挖走。河床淘沙要淘到一定深度。相传李冰在河床下埋石马，明代起改埋卧(wò)铁，作为深淘标志。"低作堰"是指飞沙堰在修筑时，不要太高，便于排洪排沙。正因为两千年来精心管理维修，都江堰才能正常工作至今。

 English Translation

Lesson Nine

The Dujiangyan

Dujiangyan is a world famous feat of water engineering not far from Chengdu in Sichuan Province. Li Bing built it during the Warring States period. In terms of age, it is as ancient as the Great Wall, but it seems that Dujiangyan has not aged through the millennia that have passed: It still fulfils its job by day and by night, irrigating several million *mu* of fertile land in the Chengdu Plain.

Before the weir existed, the Min River often flooded the land, causing loss and hardship for people in the area. Li Bing was sent to Chengdu as an official, and began the construction of dams along the Min River. He understood hydrology and found the reason for the inundations. The river has its source in the Min Mountain, and each spring, when the snow melts in the high mountains, great amounts of water descends from the heights in many streams, and they all swell the Min River. Where the river enters the plain, its bed becomes constricted and therefore high waters cause the floods. With this knowledge, Li Bing found a way to tame the river. It consists of three structures.

The first is the "Baopingkou" or "Bottleneck Channel". This structure divides the river into two at the point where it enters the plain. Part of the water is directed back to the original river bed, and the "Outer River" follows its natural course; the other into the "Inner River", a canal system that irrigates the plain. The idea is ingenious, but Yulei Hill separates the river valley from the Chengdu Plain. Li Bing decided to cut a channel through the hill. The Hill consists of hard rocks, so Li Bing let the workmen pile up brushwood and burn it, and then pour cold water on the rocks until they cracked. It took many years, but eventually they completed a 20 meters wide channel through the hill. This mouth of the irrigation system is called the "Baopingkou."

The second is the "Yuzui" or "Fish Mouse Levee". When the channel was completed, Li Bing had the "Yuzui" built in the mid-river, a dike that divides the waters and channels more water into the new riverbed. At first, the dike was built from stone, but the strong currents during high water destroyed it. Li Bing then had the idea to use large bamboo cages filled with pebbles, tied together and sunk into the river. Thus, the water-dividing dike was completed. By the principles of fluid mechanics in a curved flow, the dike directs the surface water into the "Inner River" while the deeper waters, which carry more sediment, remain in the "Outer River". By this means, the sediment charge mostly remains in the main river.

The third is the "Feishayan" or "Flying Sand Weir" in the Inner River. When the river rises too high in the high water season, the water volume exceeds the Bottleneck's capacity. At this time, the weir guides the excess water back into the main river, and thus keeps the irrigation system of the Chengdu Plain safe. In addition, it catches "sand" and thus reduces the river's sediment charge.

When the construction of the Dujiangyan was completed, the Min River no longer caused disasters, and the Chengdu Plain became an area "Country of Heaven", where "the waters follow the needs of men, knowing no hunger or famine years". The people therefore built a temple in the memory of Li Bing at the weir.

The Wonders of the Dujiangyan

Dujiangyan mainly consists of three structures, the Yuzui, the Feishayan and the Baopingkou. The first divide the river water into the Outer and the Inner River. The Outer River is the original river course, while the Inner River is the canal system used for irrigation. When water levels are low, 60% of the water of the Min River flows into the irrigation system; during high waters, 60% remains in the Outer River. It realizes the principles of fluid mechanics in a cuved flow, guiding the surface waters into the Inner River. The Feishayan stands 2.15 meters above the bed of the Inner River. When the amount of water entering the Inner River exceeds that capacity of the Baopingkou, the excess water flows back into the Outer River through the Feishayan. At extreme water levels, this weir is destroyed by the current, opening the way for the flood waters back into the main river. The Baopingkou cuts through Yulei Hill, leading the Inner River into the Chengdu Plain. During high waters, the Feishayan regulated water levels, so that the Baopingkou does not receive too great water volumes, thus maintaining the safety of the irrigation system.

The Annual Maintenance Works on the Dujiangyan

From the time when it was first built to the present day over two-thousand years have passed. Yet the Dujiangyan has never fallen into disrepair because it has been regularly repaired through all these years. In the Song period, a system for repair works that were carried out each winter to spring (the low water season) was laid down. Core works were "excavating the shoals, lowering the weir". The shoals are banks that build up in the river bed. These form after each high water season, because the river washes down great amounts of sand and rock, which build up as shoals and have to be removed to maintain a certain depth of the river bed. It is said that Li Bing had a stone horse buried in the river bottom, and iron markers were sunk in the Ming period to mark the required depth of the river. "Lowering the weir" refers to the repairs on the Feishayan that must be kept low, so that it fulfils its function of preventing floods and filtering sediment. Only because repair works have been carried out carefully every single year, the Dujiangyan still serves its function today.

第十课

中国瓷器

China，中国；china，瓷器。谈起瓷器，人们自然会想到中国。不错，世上本无瓷，瓷器是中国人发明的，中国是瓷器的故乡。

瓷器走进人类生活，算起来已有1,800多年了。现在，人们的生活几乎离不开瓷器：厨房里的瓷盘、瓷碗，客厅里的瓷花瓶，卫生间（厕所）的瓷马桶，盖房子用的瓷砖，等等。其实工业上也需要瓷器，比如飞机和航天飞行器使用的耐高温、高硬度的材料，有些就是瓷的。

那么中国人是怎么发明瓷器的呢？回答这个问题还要先从陶器说起。早在一万年前，中国人已经会制造陶器。陶器是用泥土做成盆碗，放入火中烧成的。陶器表面粗糙，吸水性强，也比较脆。

到了3,000多年前的商朝，中国人发明了"原始青瓷"。瓷器是用土做胎，在胎上涂了一种叫釉的东西，再放到1,200度的高温中去烧。瓷器坚硬，

陶瓶（距今约6,500年—5,000年）

外表光亮好看，不吸水，方便清洗。这些优点是陶器所没有的。

青瓷碗

1,800多年前（东汉），真正的青瓷终于烧制出来了。这时瓷器才算诞生了。青瓷的表面是一种淡淡的绿色或黄色，看上去光滑美丽。后来，中国人又烧出了白瓷和彩瓷。白瓷洁白如玉，烧制起来比较难。白瓷的出现很重要，因为有了白瓷才可以在瓷器表面画图画。13世纪（元朝），中国的彩瓷多起来了，其中最有名的是青花瓷。青花瓷白底蓝花，清新明快，一出现就受到人们的喜爱。

唐朝之后，中国瓷器通过陆上丝绸之路和海上丝绸之路运往中东和欧洲，很快就成了世界市场上的抢手商品。12世纪（宋朝），中国瓷器已销到日本、朝鲜、印度等五十多个国家。那时一件件精美的瓷器虽然很贵，但还是供不应求。之后，不少外国商人带着图样到中国定制瓷器。这些外销瓷无论在形状、题材和花样上都出现了异国风情。多种文化在瓷器上碰撞，新品种不断出现，中国瓷

北宋瓷器（960—1127）

更精美了。千百年来，来自各国的一艘艘商船，把中国瓷器运到了世界各地。可以说，瓷器是最早的一种世界商品。

元青花"鬼谷子下山"大罐

彩瓷

生词

cí qì 瓷器	china, porcelain	yuán shǐ 原始	primitive
chú fáng 厨房	kitchen	tāi 胎	ceramic body
kè tīng 客厅	living room	yòu 釉	glaze
cè suǒ 厕所	bathroom	yōu diǎn 优点	advantage
mǎ tǒng 马桶	toilet	dàn shēng 诞生	be born
gài 盖	build, construct	shì chǎng 市场	market
cí zhuān 瓷砖	porcelain tile	xiāo 销	sell, trade
gēng yè 工业	industry	tí cái 题材	motif
xū yào 需要	need, demand	yì 异	other, foreign
táo qì 陶器	pottery	pèng zhuàng 碰撞	encounter, meet
cuì 脆	brittle		

听写

瓷器　厨房　客厅　厕所　瓷砖　工业　需要　脆

优点　诞生　市场　销　*胎　釉

比一比

$$\begin{cases} 次（一次）\\ 瓷（瓷器）\end{cases} \qquad \begin{cases} 消（消息）\\ 销（销售）\end{cases}$$

$$\begin{cases} 台（舞台）\\ 胎（胎儿）\end{cases} \qquad \begin{cases} 危（危险）\\ 脆（脆弱）\end{cases}$$

销

反义词

优点——缺点　　　　诞生——死亡

多音字

jī 　　　　　　　jǐ
几 　　　　　　　几
jī 　　　　　　　jǐ
几乎　　　　　　　几个

词语运用

需要

① 我做中文作业,需要一本中文字典。

② 当飞行员需要眼睛好。

③ 医生对病人说:"你需要休息一段时间。"

供不应求

① 来这家商店买手机的人常常要排队,真是供不应求。

② 大龙虾在市场上很受欢迎,常常供不应求。

词语解释

供不应求——提供的东西不能满足需要

外销瓷——卖到国外的瓷器

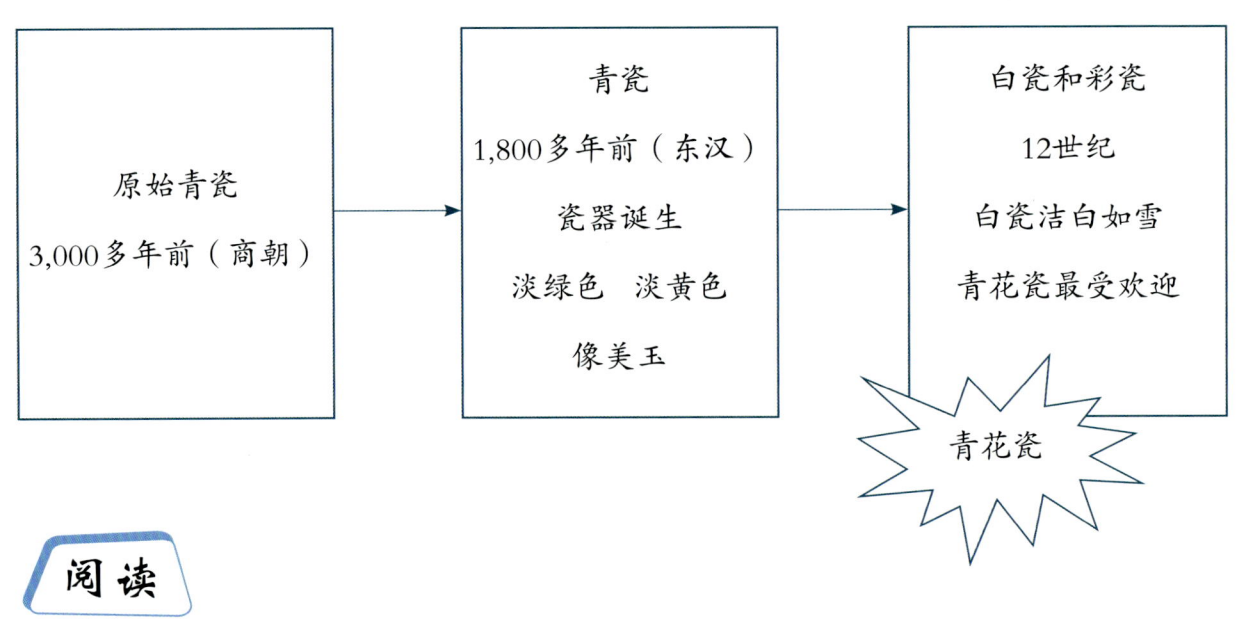

阅读

瓷行天下——外销瓷

清雍正徽章纹盘（约1735）

中国瓷器的历史，一定少不了外销瓷。唐代以后中国瓷器走向世界时，遇到了一个问题：世界很大，文化多种多样，外国人虽然喜欢中国瓷器，但他们有自己的生活习惯、宗(zōng)教和审(shěn)美要求。比如中东人的清真寺(sì)、民居常用蓝色装饰，而欧洲贵族呢，希望瓷器上有家族的族徽(huī)。明中期以后，一些外国商人带来欧洲图案(àn)样品，定制中国瓷器，数量巨大。很快中国外销瓷的题材和花样出现了异国风情。16—18世纪，中国外销瓷器多达3亿件。

清乾隆"圣经故事"鼻烟盒

1785年清乾隆西洋行猎碗

青花瓷

青花瓷源于中国。13世纪（元朝），彩瓷多了起来。彩瓷中青花瓷色白花青，质朴大方，最为抢眼。生产青花，首先要能生产白瓷，还需要钴料的宝石蓝发色。元代景德镇用高岭土生产出了白如玉、明如镜的白瓷，又因元朝时波斯的颜料（钴料）输往中国，在中国工匠的手中，高品质的青花瓷被生产出来，销到世界各地，被人们宠爱。

元青花菱花式大盘

元青花"萧何月下追韩信"梅瓶

资料

瓷都景德镇

景德镇位于中国江西，是一个很有特色的城市，整座城市"瓷味"十足，就连街道两旁的路灯杆，都用陶瓷做成。景德镇有两千多年的制陶史，瓷器的制造和火热的瓷器交易已有千年。1278年，元朝在景德镇设立浮梁瓷局，管理制瓷业。三百年前，一位法国人来到景德镇，他看到这里处处是瓷窑(yáo)，一股股的烟飘着；夜晚瓷窑火光通明，炉工在照看着炉火。在景德镇，清朝时已有官窑三千多个。这里的男女老少，大多以瓷为业。自古以来，景德镇汇(huì)集了顶尖的工匠，他们制造瓷器过程十分严(yán)格，一件瓷器要过几十道手才能完成。景德镇精美的瓷器，实现了"点土成金"的神话。

景德镇

Lesson Ten

Chinese Porcelain

Have you ever wondered why China and china are the same word? You might think that china has something to do with China. That is quite correct because porcelain originated in China.

Some 1,800 years ago, porcelain first entered the lives of human beings. Nowadays, we can handily do without: china dishes and china bowls in our kitchens, porcelain vases in our living rooms, porcelain toilets in our bathrooms, and china tiles on our roofs, to name just a few. And the industry also needs porcelain where high temperature resistance and hardness is required, such as in certain parts of airplanes and space shuttles.

So how was porcelain invented? To answer this question, we have to start with pottery. The use of pottery in China began ten thousand years ago. Pottery is made by shaping clay, for instance into bowls, and then firing them. Low-fired pottery is relatively rough on the surface, absorbs water, and not very hard.

During the Shang period some 3,000 years ago, Chinese potters invented "primitive green wares". They shaped the bodies of their vessels from clay, added a layer of glaze on the surface, and fired the product at up to 1,200℃. This stoneware was hard and had a shiny surface. Because it absorbed no liquids, it was easily cleaned. It thus had advantages over ordinary pottery.

Some 1,800 years ago during the Eastern Han, the first true porcelain appeared. It is called "green ware" for its light greenish or yellowish color, and prized for its smooth surface and beautiful appearance. Later on, other potters invented white wares and colorful wares. Pure white porcelain rivals jade in beauty, yet making it was difficult. White wares were particularly important because the pure white bodies were ideal for colorful motifs. In the Yuan period in the thirteenth century, colorful wares multiplied, with blue and white wares the most famous. Blue and white ware has painted blue motifs on the white ground; the clean and fresh appearance of this porcelain was an instant success.

From the Tang period, china was exported by the overland and the maritime Silk Roads, reaching the Middle East and Europe, and it was soon in great demand wherever it became available. In the twelfth century during the Song period, porcelain was regularly traded to Japan, Korea, India and some fifty other countries. In this period, a beautiful piece of china cost a fortune, yet demand exceeded supply. Later on, merchants from abroad bought designs for their orders, introducing shapes, forms and motifs of their countries. Inputs of many cultures met in the porcelain industry, inducing the creation of new wares and enriching the beauty of Chinese porcelains. For many centuries, merchant ships from all over the world carried china to every corner of the globe. Porcelain may be called the first mass-produced global good.

Porcelain for the World: Chinese Export Wares

In the history of Chinese porcelain, the export wares are an interesting chapter. From the Tang period, when exports began, traders encountered a problem: In the wide world with its many cultures, many liked china, but had their own ideas defined by their customs, religions and aesthetics. Thus, people in the Middle East liked blue in their mosques and houses, while European nobles liked their coat of arms on their china plates. From the mid-Ming, some foreign merchants brought designs from Europe that they wished to have produced in China. Export wares with non-Chinese motifs soon appeared, and they sold in huge quantities. From the sixteenth through the eighteenth centuries, about 300 million pieces of export wares were made!

Blue and White Wares

Blue and white porcelain originated in China. In the thirteenth century during the Yuan period, when colorful wares became common, blue motifs on white ground stood out for their simple elegance. This used pure white porcelain for the body, with the motifs painted in cobalt blue. In the Yuan period, the Jingdezhen kilns produced a near transparent white porcelain from Gaoling clay. And the Yuan empire had access to import cobalt from distant Persia, skillful Chinese artisans produced the finest blue and white wares, which were exported all around the globe and much appreciated everywhere.

The China Capital Jingdezhen

Jingdezhen is in the center of Jiangxi Province and a very special city that "smells" of porcelain throughout. Even the street lamp poles are made from it! Jingdezhen looks back on two millennia of ceramic production and the porcelain industry here with its busy trade is a thousand years old.

In 1278, the Yuan dynasty set up the Fuliang porcelain office to supervise production. Three-hundred years ago, a Frenchman visited Jingdezhen and saw kilns and smoke everywhere, an industrial center busy around the clock, the kilns glowing red in the night and many workers busy looking after them. At the time, the Qing dynasty operated more than three thousand government kilns. Almost everyone, men and women, old and young, worked in the industry. Jingdezhen always attracted the best craftsmen and they maintained the highest standards in every step in the production. Each piece that left the kilns had passed through several dozen skilled hands. The beautiful wares of Jingdezhen realized the saying of "turning mud into gold by touching".

选修课

张衡和他的地动仪

晚上，满天的星星像无数珍珠挂在天空。一个孩子坐在院子里，仰着头，指着天空数星星。一颗，两颗……一直数到了几百颗。奶奶笑着说："傻孩子，又在数星星了。那么多星星，一闪一闪地乱动，眼都花了。你能数得清吗？"孩子说："奶奶，能看得见，就能数得清。星星是动，可不是乱动。您看，这颗星和那颗星，它们离得总是一样远。"

张衡

爷爷走过来说："孩子，你看得很仔细。天上的星星是在动，可是，他们之间的距离是不变的。我们的祖先把它们分成一组一组的，还给他们起了名字。"爷爷停了停，指着北边的天空，说："你看，那七颗星，连起来像一把勺子，叫北斗星。离它们不远的那颗星，叫北极星。北斗星总是绕着北极星转。"

爷爷说的话是真的吗？这孩子一夜没睡好，几次起来看星星。他看清楚了，北斗星果然绕着北极星慢慢转动。

这个数星星的孩子叫张衡（78—139），是汉朝人。

他长大以后发明了地动仪和浑天仪，成为一位伟大的天文学家。张衡的地动仪，造于公元132年，是世界上最早的测定地震方位的仪器。地动仪是用铜制造的，上面有八条龙，分别朝着八个方向。每条龙的嘴里含着一个小铜球。哪个方向发生地震，哪个方向的龙就吐出铜球，落在下面的青蛙嘴里。浑天仪是演示日月星辰运行的仪器。

公元138年的一天，突然地动仪朝西的龙吐出铜球，落入青蛙嘴里。过了几天，洛阳西边一千里远的陇(lǒng)西派人送来消息，那里发生了地震。地动仪测出的地震方向和时间都是对的。

河南南阳张衡博物馆

生词

zhāng héng 张衡	Zhang Heng, *a name*	tiān wén xué 天文学	astronomy
zhēn zhū 珍珠	pearl	cè dìng 测定	measure
yǎng 仰	look up	hán 含	hold, contain
jù lí 距离	distance	yǎn shì 演示	show, demonstrate
zǔ xiān 祖先	ancestor	yùn xíng 运行	move along a defined path
běi dǒu xīng 北斗星	the Big Dipper	luò yáng 洛阳	Luoyang (*the capital of the Eastern Han*)
hún tiān yí 浑天仪	armillary sphere		

听写

珍珠　仰　距离　祖先　北斗星　天文学　测定

演示

比一比

$$\begin{cases} 祖（祖先）\\ 组（小组）\end{cases} \qquad 演\begin{cases} 演示\\ 表演\end{cases}$$

$$离\begin{cases} 距离\\ 离开\end{cases} \qquad 珍\begin{cases} 珍珠\\ 珍稀\end{cases}$$

词语运用

数学　数一数

① 张春明非常喜欢数学。

② 熊妈妈说："小黑熊，快把地里的玉米数一数！"

乱动　刮风

① 上课时要坐好，不要乱动。

② 北京的春天常常刮大风。

儿子　仔细

① 爸爸让儿子帮助妈妈干活。

② 读书要仔细，不要马虎。

词语解释

陇西——地理名词，指甘肃省陇西县

阅读

祖冲之

中国古代有一位著名的科学家叫祖冲之（429—500）。他计算出圆周率（π）在3.1415926到3.1415927之间，第一次把圆周率推算到小数点后七位。一千年以后，阿拉伯数学家才算出比祖冲之的计算更精确的圆周率。

祖冲之

 *English Translation*

Elective Course

Zhang Heng and His Seismoscope

In the evening, countless stars appear in the sky. A little boy was sitting in the courtyard, looking up at the sky and counting the stars, one, two, until he had counted to several hundred. His grandmother laughed: "Silly child, there you are again counting the stars. They blink, they hop around, you'll wreck your eyes. Can you ever count them all?" The child answered: "If you could see them all, you could count them all. The stars move, but not move randomly. Look at that two, they are always at the same distance."

His grandfather came over: "My boy, you are paying attention. The stars are moving, but the distance among them does not change. Our ancestors organized them in groups, and the groups have names." He stopped to point out the Big Dipper in the sky: "Look, the seven stars, if you connect them you get the shape of a ladle, this is the Big Dipper. And that star not far is the Polaris. The Big Dipper always turns around the Polaris."

Was grandfather right? The boy hardly slept that night, getting up time and again to look at the stars. And he saw clearly, the Big Dipper slowly revolves around the Pole Star!

The boy who liked looking at the stars was Zhang Heng (78—139). He lived in the Eastern Han period.

As an adult, he invented the seismometer and the armillary sphere and became a great astronomer. He made the seismometer in 132. It is the first mechanical device that measures the direction of an earthquake. The seismometer is a bronze vessel with eight dragons mounted on the wall, facing in the different directions. Each dragon holds a small bronze ball in its mouth. When an earthquake occurs, the dragon pointing in the direction of the earthquake will drop its ball into the open mouth of the frog below. The armillary sphere is a model that shows the movements of the sun, the moon, and the stars.

One day in 138, the dragon on the seismometer that faced west dropped its ball into the frog's mouth. A few days later, a messenger from Longxi, a region 1000 *li* west of Luoyang, arrived to report an earthquake. The seismometer had correctly shown the direction of the earthquake.

Zu Chongzhi

Zu Chongzhi was a famous scientist of old China (429-500). He calculated that the mathematical constant π is between 3.1415926 and 3.1415927. He was the first to calculate the circumference rate to seven digits after the full number. A thousand years passed until Arabic mathematicians worked this constant out with greater exactness than Zu Chongzhi.

生字表（简）

1. tāng sháo cí báo tiě āo āi gāng pèi luó wù chū cù
   汤 勺 磁 薄 铁 凹 挨 钢 配 罗 雾 初 促
   háng
   航

2. cài lún bó xù cāo gùn jiē yàn jiāng mò ā
   蔡 伦 帛 絮 糙 棍 揭 验 浆 墨 阿

3. liàn kuàng lú bào zhà tàn lì hùn wèi wǔ fǎng qiāng
   炼 矿 炉 爆 炸 炭 例 混 未 武 坊 枪
   gōng
   供

4. chāo sù diāo bǎn bì jiàng fèi bǔ chāi là zhān pào jiāo
   抄 速 雕 版 毕 匠 废 补 拆 蜡 粘 泡 胶
   gǎo yā
   稿 压

5. chóu juàn shuì fǎng sù shā kè shì wén cè mì páo
   绸 绢 税 纺 素 纱 克 式 纹 侧 秘 袍
   hōng jià áng
   轰 价 昂

6. suí shè jì wǎ jiàng fù zhǎng láo dūn gǒng huǎn wān
   隋 设 计 瓦 匠 傅 涨 牢 墩 拱 缓 弯
   zhèn kuà
   震 跨

7. biǎn què zhěn diàn jī dàn wēn yì qū guǐ jiǔ tāng
   扁 鹊 诊 奠 基 旦 瘟 疫 驱 鬼 灸 汤
   liáo mài wèi suǐ
   疗 脉 胃 髓

8. 纲(gāng) 误(wù) 漏(lòu) 渣(zhā) 铺(pù) 廷(tíng) 阅(yuè) 籍(jí) 订(dìng) 科(kē) 制(zhì) 卷(juàn) 译(yì)

9. 堰(yàn) 坝(bà) 昼(zhòu) 溉(gài) 亩(mǔ) 岷(mín) 窄(zhǎi) 股(gǔ) 垒(lěi) 劈(pī) 坚(jiān) 瓶(píng) 垮(kuǎ) 笼(lóng) 荒(huāng)

10. 瓷(cí) 厨(chú) 厕(cè) 盖(gài) 砖(zhuān) 需(xū) 陶(táo) 脆(cuì) 胎(tāi) 釉(yòu) 优(yōu) 诞(dàn) 销(xiāo) 异(yì)

选修课 衡(héng) 仰(yǎng) 距(jù) 祖(zǔ) 浑(hún) 仪(yí) 测(cè) 含(hán) 洛(luò)

共计 149 个生字

生字表（繁）

1. 湯(tāng) 勺(sháo) 磁(cí) 薄(báo) 鐵(tiě) 凹(āo) 挨(āi) 鋼(gāng) 配(pèi) 羅(luó) 霧(wù) 初(chū) 促(cù)
   航(háng)

2. 蔡(cài) 倫(lún) 帛(bó) 絮(xù) 糙(cāo) 棍(gùn) 揭(jiē) 驗(yàn) 漿(jiāng) 墨(mò) 阿(ā)

3. 煉(liàn) 礦(kuàng) 爐(lú) 爆(bào) 炸(zhà) 炭(tàn) 例(lì) 混(hùn) 未(wèi) 武(wǔ) 坊(fǎng) 槍(qiāng)
   供(gōng)

4. 抄(chāo) 速(sù) 雕(diāo) 版(bǎn) 畢(bì) 匠(jiàng) 廢(fèi) 補(bǔ) 拆(chāi) 蠟(là) 粘(zhān) 泡(pào) 膠(jiāo)
   稿(gǎo) 壓(yā)

5. 綢(chóu) 絹(juàn) 稅(shuì) 紡(fǎng) 素(sù) 紗(shā) 克(kè) 式(shì) 紋(wén) 側(cè) 秘(mì) 袍(páo)
   轟(hōng) 價(jià) 昂(áng)

6. 隋(suí) 設(shè) 計(jì) 瓦(wǎ) 匠(jiàng) 傅(fù) 漲(zhǎng) 牢(láo) 墩(dūn) 拱(gǒng) 緩(huǎn) 彎(wān)
   震(zhèn) 跨(kuà)

7. 扁(biǎn) 鵲(què) 診(zhěn) 奠(diàn) 基(jī) 旦(dàn) 瘟(wēn) 疫(yì) 驅(qū) 鬼(guǐ) 灸(jiǔ) 湯(tāng)
   療(liáo) 脈(mài) 胃(wèi) 髓(suǐ)

8. 綱(gāng) 誤(wù) 漏(lòu) 渣(zhā) 鋪(pù) 廷(tíng) 閱(yuè) 籍(jí) 訂(dìng) 科(kē) 製(zhì) 卷(juàn) 譯(yì)

9. 堰(yàn) 壩(bà) 晝(zhòu) 溉(gài) 畝(mǔ) 岷(mín) 窄(zhǎi) 股(gǔ) 壘(lěi) 劈(pī) 堅(jiān) 瓶(píng) 垮(kuǎ) 籠(lóng) 荒(huāng)

10. 瓷(cí) 廚(chú) 厠(cè) 蓋(gài) 磚(zhuān) 需(xū) 陶(táo) 脆(cuì) 胎(tāi) 釉(yòu) 優(yōu) 誕(dàn) 銷(xiāo) 異(yì)

选修课 衡(héng) 仰(yǎng) 距(jù) 祖(zǔ) 渾(hún) 儀(yí) 測(cè) 含(hán) 洛(luò)

共計 149 個生字

生词表（简）

1. tāng sháo 汤勺　cí 磁　fāng wèi 方位　zì yóu 自由　báo 薄　tiě 铁　āo 凹　āi 挨　zhǐ shì 指示　gāng 钢　pèi 配
   luó pán 罗盘　shì jì 世纪　wù 雾　mí shī 迷失　ān quán 安全　chū 初　cù jìn 促进　háng hǎi 航海

2. cài lún 蔡伦　zhú jiǎn 竹简　bèn zhòng 笨重　bào gào 报告　bó 帛　sī xù 丝絮　má 麻　cū cāo 粗糙　gùn zi 棍子
   sī mián 丝绵　jiē 揭　shēng chǎn 生产　yú wǎng 渔网　pò bù 破布　yuán liào 原料　shì yàn 试验　jiāng 浆　mò 墨
   lǐ xiǎng 理想　ā lā bó 阿拉伯

3. huǒ yào 火药　yān huā 烟花　liàn dān 炼丹　kuàng 矿　lú 炉　bào zhà 爆炸　mù tàn 木炭　àn zhào 按照　bǐ lì 比例
   hùn hé 混合　yì wài 意外　qián suǒ wèi yǒu 前所未有　lì liàng 力量　wǔ qì 武器　zuò zhàn 作战　zhèng fǔ 政府　zuò fang 作坊
   qiāng 枪　zǐ dàn 子弹　gōng 供

4. yìn shuā 印刷　chāo xiě 抄写　sù dù 速度　diāo bǎn 雕版　bì shēng 毕升　gōng jiàng 工匠　zuò fèi 作废　bǔ 补　chāi kāi 拆开
   là 蜡　zhān 粘　pào 泡　jiāo ní 胶泥　jiē shi 结实　gǎo jiàn 稿件　yā píng 压平

5. sī chóu 丝绸　juàn 绢　yòng tú 用途　gōng zī 工资　jiāo shuì 交税　róu ruǎn 柔软　fǎng zhī 纺织　sù shā 素纱　kè 克
   gè shì gè yàng 各式各样　huā wén 花纹　cè kàn 侧看　shén mì 神秘　chǎn pǐn 产品　sī páo 丝袍　hōng dòng 轰动
   zhuī pěng 追捧　jià gé 价格　áng guì 昂贵　shí shàng jiè 时尚界

6. 隋朝（suí cháo） 设计（shè jì） 瓦匠（wǎ jiàng） 师傅（shī fu） 请教（qǐng jiào） 涨水（zhǎng shuǐ） 牢固（láo gù） 桥墩（qiáo dūn） 拱形（gǒng xíng） 结构（jié gòu） 冲力（chōng lì） 节省（jié shěng） 平缓（píng huǎn） 美观（měi guān） 弯（wān） 地震（dì zhèn） 横跨（héng kuà） 过往（guò wǎng）

7. 扁鹊（biǎn què） 诊（zhěn） 奠基（diàn jī） 一旦（yí dàn） 瘟疫（wēn yì） 流行（liú xíng） 驱鬼（qū guǐ） 针灸（zhēn jiǔ） 汤药（tāng yào） 治疗（zhì liáo） 血脉（xuè mài） 肠胃（cháng wèi） 骨髓（gǔ suǐ） 触摸（chù mō） 医疗（yī liáo） 理论（lǐ lùn） 经验（jīng yàn）

8. 纲目（gāng mù） 家庭（jiā tíng） 错误（cuò wù） 漏写（lòu xiě） 药方（yào fāng） 药渣（yào zhā） 药铺（yào pù） 朝廷（cháo tíng） 阅读（yuè dú） 典籍（diǎn jí） 校订（jiào dìng） 疑问（yí wèn） 收集（shōu jí） 科学（kē xué） 形态（xíng tài） 制作（zhì zuò） 附上（fù shang） 卷（juàn） 翻译（fān yì）

9. 都江堰（dū jiāng yàn） 坝（bà） 水利工程（shuǐ lì gōng chéng） 昼夜（zhòu yè） 灌溉（guàn gài） 亩（mǔ） 岷江（mín jiāng） 窄（zhǎi） 股（gǔ） 垒（lěi） 劈开（pī kāi） 坚硬（jiān yìng） 瓶（píng） 冲垮（chōng kuǎ） 笼（lóng） 荒年（huāng nián）

10. 瓷器（cí qì） 厨房（chú fáng） 客厅（kè tīng） 厕所（cè suǒ） 马桶（mǎ tǒng） 盖（gài） 瓷砖（cí zhuān） 工业（gēng yè） 需要（xū yào） 陶器（táo qì） 脆（cuì） 原始（yuán shǐ） 胎（tāi） 釉（yòu） 优点（yōu diǎn） 诞生（dàn shēng） 市场（shì chǎng） 销（xiāo） 题材（tí cái） 异（yì） 碰撞（pèng zhuàng）

选修课 张衡（zhāng héng） 珍珠（zhēn zhū） 仰（yǎng） 距离（jù lí） 祖先（zǔ xiān） 北斗星（běi dǒu xīng） 浑天仪（hún tiān yí） 天文学（tiān wén xué） 测定（cè dìng） 含（hán） 演示（yǎn shì） 运行（yùn xíng） 洛阳（luò yáng）

共计 199 个生词

生词表（繁）

1. 湯勺 (tāng sháo) 磁 (cí) 方位 (fāng wèi) 自由 (zì yóu) 薄 (báo) 鐵 (tiě) 凹 (āo) 挨 (āi) 指示 (zhǐ shì) 鋼 (gāng) 配 (pèi)
羅盤 (luó pán) 世紀 (shì jì) 霧 (wù) 迷失 (mí shī) 安全 (ān quán) 初 (chū) 促進 (cù jìn) 航海 (háng hǎi)

2. 蔡倫 (cài lún) 竹簡 (zhú jiǎn) 笨重 (bèn zhòng) 報告 (bào gào) 帛 (bó) 絲絮 (sī xù) 麻 (má) 粗糙 (cū cāo) 棍子 (gùn zi)
絲綿 (sī mián) 揭 (jiē) 生產 (shēng chǎn) 漁網 (yú wǎng) 破布 (pò bù) 原料 (yuán liào) 試驗 (shì yàn) 漿 (jiāng) 墨 (mò)
理想 (lǐ xiǎng) 阿拉伯 (ā lā bó)

3. 火藥 (huǒ yào) 煙花 (yān huā) 煉丹 (liàn dān) 礦 (kuàng) 爐 (lú) 爆炸 (bào zhà) 木炭 (mù tàn) 按照 (àn zhào) 比例 (bǐ lì)
混合 (hùn hé) 意外 (yì wài) 前所未有 (qián suǒ wèi yǒu) 力量 (lì liàng) 武器 (wǔ qì) 作戰 (zuò zhàn) 政府 (zhèng fǔ) 作坊 (zuò fang)
槍 (qiāng) 子彈 (zǐ dàn) 供 (gōng)

4. 印刷 (yìn shuā) 抄寫 (chāo xiě) 速度 (sù dù) 雕版 (diāo bǎn) 畢昇 (bì shēng) 工匠 (gōng jiàng) 作廢 (zuò fèi) 補 (bǔ) 拆開 (chāi kāi)
蠟 (là) 粘 (zhān) 泡 (pào) 膠泥 (jiāo ní) 結實 (jiē shi) 稿件 (gǎo jiàn) 壓平 (yā píng)

5. 絲綢 (sī chóu) 絹 (juàn) 用途 (yòng tú) 工資 (gōng zī) 交稅 (jiāo shuì) 柔軟 (róu ruǎn) 紡織 (fǎng zhī) 素紗 (sù shā) 克 (kè)
各式各樣 (gè shì gè yàng) 花紋 (huā wén) 側看 (cè kàn) 神秘 (shén mì) 產品 (chǎn pǐn) 絲袍 (sī páo) 轟動 (hōng dòng)
追捧 (zhuī pěng) 價格 (jià gé) 昂貴 (áng guì) 時尚界 (shí shàng jiè)

6. 隋朝（suí cháo） 設計（shè jì） 瓦匠（wǎ jiàng） 師傅（shī fu） 請教（qǐng jiào） 漲水（zhǎng shuǐ） 牢固（láo gù） 橋墩（qiáo dūn） 拱形（gǒng xíng） 結構（jié gòu） 沖力（chōng lì） 節省（jié shěng） 平緩（píng huǎn） 美觀（měi guān） 彎（wān） 地震（dì zhèn） 橫跨（héng kuà） 過往（guò wǎng）

7. 扁鵲（biǎn què） 診（zhěn） 奠基（diàn jī） 一旦（yí dàn） 瘟疫（wēn yì） 流行（liú xíng） 驅鬼（qū guǐ） 針灸（zhēn jiǔ） 湯藥（tāng yào） 治療（zhì liáo） 血脈（xuè mài） 腸胃（cháng wèi） 骨髓（gǔ suǐ） 觸摸（chù mō） 醫療（yī liáo） 理論（lǐ lùn） 經驗（jīng yàn）

8. 綱目（gāng mù） 家庭（jiā tíng） 錯誤（cuò wù） 漏寫（lòu xiě） 藥方（yào fāng） 藥渣（yào zhā） 藥鋪（yào pù） 朝廷（cháo tíng） 閱讀（yuè dú） 典籍（diǎn jí） 校訂（jiào dìng） 疑問（yí wèn） 收集（shōu jí） 科學（kē xué） 形態（xíng tài） 製作（zhì zuò） 附上（fù shang） 卷（juàn） 翻譯（fān yì）

9. 都江堰（dū jiāng yàn） 壩（bà） 水利工程（shuǐ lì gōng chéng） 晝夜（zhòu yè） 灌溉（guàn gài） 畝（mǔ） 岷江（mín jiāng） 窄（zhǎi） 股（gǔ） 壘（lěi） 劈開（pī kāi） 堅硬（jiān yìng） 瓶（píng） 沖垮（chōng kuǎ） 籠（lóng） 荒年（huāng nián）

10. 瓷器（cí qì） 廚房（chú fáng） 客廳（kè tīng） 廁所（cè suǒ） 馬桶（mǎ tǒng） 蓋（gài） 瓷磚（cí zhuān） 工業（gēng yè） 需要（xū yào） 陶器（táo qì） 脆（cuì） 原始（yuán shǐ） 胎（tāi） 釉（yòu） 優點（yōu diǎn） 誕生（dàn shēng） 市場（shì chǎng） 銷（xiāo） 題材（tí cái） 異（yì） 碰撞（pèng zhuàng）

選修課 張衡（zhāng héng） 珍珠（zhēn zhū） 仰（yǎng） 距離（jù lí） 祖先（zǔ xiān） 北斗星（běi dǒu xīng） 渾天儀（hún tiān yí） 天（tiān） 文學（wén xué） 測定（cè dìng） 含（hán） 演示（yǎn shì） 運行（yùn xíng） 洛陽（luò yáng）

共計 199 個生詞

附录

"新双双中文教材"写作练习（1—10册）

课文正式教授写作内容

内容	出处	建议学习年级
1. 课文缩写	第4册 "猴子捞月亮"	3—4年级
2. 日记	第5册 "妈妈教我写日记"	4—5年级
3. 叙事文	第5册 "参观兵马俑"	4—5年级
4. 看图写故事	第6册 《中国成语故事》"塞翁失马"	5—6年级
5. 城市介绍	第7册 《中国地理常识》"著名城市"	5—6年级
6. 书信	第8册 《中国古代故事》"七步诗"	5—6年级
7. 写人	第9册 《中国神话传说》"嫦娥奔月"	6—7年级

辅助写作练习

内容	出处	建议学习年级
1. 读书笔记	亲子阅读，每周家庭读书、写作	2—6年级
2. 观察记录	第4册 写"养蚕报告"	3—4年级
3. 创作	写简单的故事和想法	4年级以上

新双双中文教材 10
New Chinese Language and Culture Course

中国古代科学技术
Ancient Chinese Science and Technology

练习本　单课　

（第二版）

［美］王双双　编著

北京大学出版社
PEKING UNIVERSITY PRESS

NanHai
BRIDGING EAST & WEST

目 录

第一课　　四大发明（一）指南针 …………………………………… 1

第三课　　四大发明（三）火药 ……………………………………… 6

第五课　　丝　绸 ……………………………………………………… 11

第七课　　扁鹊的四诊法 ……………………………………………… 16

第九课　　都江堰 ……………………………………………………… 22

第一课
四大发明（一）指南针

一　写生词

磁					
薄					
铁					
凹					
挨					
钢					
配					
雾					
初					
汤	勺				

方	位				
自	由				
指	示				
罗	盘				
世	纪				
迷	失				
安	全				
促	进				
航	海				

二　下列汉字是由哪些部分组成的

磁 → ☐ + ☐　　　　雾 → ☐ + ☐

示 → ☐ + ☐　　　　雷 → ☐ + ☐

第一课 四大发明（一）指南针

三 组词

航空公司　磁铁　表示　钢铁

铁 { _____

磁 { _____

示 { _____

航 { _____

四 选字组词

（足　促）进　　（航　船）海　　打（雷　雾）

（足　促）球　　（航　船）长　　下（雷　雾）

五 看图连线

公司　　　　司南　　　　司机

第一课
四大发明（一）指南针

六　反义词

薄 —— _____　　　　　　天然 —— _____

七　给下面的字加拼音，哪个字最好记？请在字上打个√

薄 _____　　　凹 _____　　　配 _____

八　朗读下面两句话，背下来

> 指南针可以指示方向。
> 指南针促进了航海业的发展。

九　选择填空

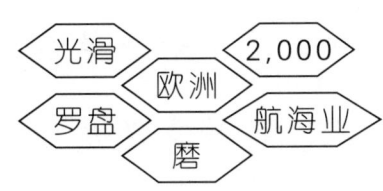

1. 大约在_____多年前的战国时期，中国人就发现磁石可以用来指方向。

2. 中国人把天然磁石磨成一个_____的小勺，放在一个写有方位的盘子上，让它自由转动。

3. 人们把钢针放在磁石上_____，使钢针变成了磁针。

第一课
四大发明（一）指南针

4. 12世纪中国的海船上就装有_____。

5. 13世纪初，中国的指南针传到_____。

6. 指南针大大促进了世界_____的发展。

十 根据课文判断对错

1. 中国最早的指南针是春秋时期的司南。　　　　　　___对___错

2. 司南是由用磁石做成的小勺和写有方位的盘子组成的。　　　　　　　　　　　　　　　　　　　　___对___错

3. 磁针和有方位的盘一起组成了罗盘。　　　　　　___对___错

4. 阴雨、大雾天气，有了罗盘，船就不会迷失方向。___对___错

5. 罗盘可以准确地指方向。　　　　　　　　　　　___对___错

十一 选择填空

1. 不管是苹果还是香蕉，_____。　　　　都没我长得高

2. 不管是哥哥还是姐姐，_____。　　　　他都喜欢

3. 不管是足球还是篮球，_____。　　　　我都爱吃

十二 造句

不管……还是……_____

安全_____

第一课
四大发明（一）指南针

十三 ‖阅读作业‖

（一）根据《磁石的故事》判断对错

1. 2,000多年前，中国人就知道磁石可以吸铁。　　＿＿对＿＿错

2. 秦始皇不怕有人带武器伤害他。　　＿＿对＿＿错

3. 带着剑的刺客到了宫门，剑被吸住了。　　＿＿对＿＿错

4. 刺客杀死了秦始皇。　　＿＿对＿＿错

（二）请按要求画出2张草图

司南	细线挂着的磁针和写有方位的盘一起组成真正的指南针

十四　读课文两遍

第三课
四大发明（三）火药

一 写生词

矿					
炉					
枪					
供					
火	药				
烟	花				
炼	丹				
爆	炸				
木	炭				
按	照				

比	例				
混	合				
意	外				
力	量				
武	器				
作	战				
政	府				
作	坊				
子	弹				
前	所	未	有		

二 组新字

山 + 灰 ⟶ ☐ 　　土 + 方 ⟶ ☐

火 + 因 ⟶ ☐ 　　火 + 户 ⟶ ☐

石 + 广 ⟶ ☐ 　　正 + 文 ⟶ ☐

第三课
四大发明（三）火药

三 选字组词

（炸 昨）天　　下（例 列）　　（混 棍）子

爆（炸 昨）　　比（例 列）　　（混 棍）合

四 写拼音

混 _____　　炸 _____　　例 _____
棍 _____　　昨 _____　　列 _____

五 在下列方框中圈出11个词，并写出来

爆	例	竹	坊	烟	作	器	力
花	昨	火	器	政	府	量	混
武	比	丹	药	武	爆	采	正
量	炸	府	炼	竹	比	例	矿
合	烟	炼	列	炸	武	混	比
力	花	作	爆	器	炼	药	合
矿	药	丹	坊	采	丹	合	棍

_____　_____
_____　_____
_____　_____
_____　_____
_____　_____
_____

第三课 四大发明（三）火药

六 将方框中的词语与合适的解释连线

色彩缤纷	从来没有发生过的
前所未有	颜色多，非常好看
意外	国家社会管理的机关
政府	意料之外，料想不到

七 选词填空

1. 春节时中国人要放烟花和_____。（爆竹　爆炸）

2. 美丽的烟花和爆竹是用_____制成的。（火药　中药）

3. 道士想炼仙药，却意外地发明了_____。（火药　中药）

4. 火药可以用来开山_____。（采矿　采花）

5. 火药，使人类得到了一种巨大的_____。（重量　力量）

6. 很快，火药就被用在_____上。（考试　武器）

八 根据课文判断对错

1. 火药是中国人最早发明的。　　　　　　　　　　　____对____错

2. 火药发明的时间大约在1,500年前的明朝。　　　　____对____错

3. 中国古代的火药武器有火药箭、火球等。　　　　　____对____错

第三课
四大发明（三）火药

4. 宋朝政府有火药作坊，不断发明各种火器。　　　____对____错

5. 宋朝一次作战就用了25支火药箭。　　　　　　　____对____错

6. 火药传入了印度后，又传入阿拉伯和欧洲。　　　____对____错

九　造句

按照_____

意外_____

十　学完本课，写一写你最有兴趣的内容（不少于6句）

第三课
四大发明（三）火药

十一 ‖阅读作业‖

根据《炼丹与火药》《勇敢的万户》判断对错

1. 道士想炼仙丹，却意外地发明了火药。　　　　____对____错

2. 500年前，中国的万户用火药做了一次"飞天"的试验。

　　　　　　　　　　　　　　　　　　　　　　____对____错

3. 万户在椅子后面装了火药，手是空的。　　　　____对____错

4. 万户失败了，但是他的想法有道理。　　　　　____对____错

十二 选做题

问：世界那么大，为什么中国人最早发明了火药？

答：一种说法是：火药需要的硝石比较少见，而中国有很多硝石矿。硝石矿的形成又与中国的气候有关系。想研究一下吗？

第五课 丝绸

一 写生词

绢					
克					
丝	绸				
用	途				
工	资				
交	税				
柔	软				
纺	织				
素	纱				
花	纹				
侧	看				

神	秘				
产	品				
丝	袍				
轰	动				
追	捧				
价	格				
昂	贵				
时	尚	界			
各	式	各	样		

二 选方框中合适的字组词

交 格 花 贵 追 品

昂_____   税_____   价_____

捧_____   产_____   纹_____

第五课 丝绸

三 选字组词

（袍 跑）了　　（柔 矛）软　　（当 挡）住

（袍 跑）子　　（柔 矛）盾　　（当 挡）然

四 写拼音，再组词

矛 _____ _____
柔 _____ _____

上 _____ _____
尚 _____ _____

五 写出反义词

昂贵 —— _____　　神秘 —— _____

六 选词填空

1. 在马王堆的_____中，发现了精美的丝织品。（汉墓　汉朝）

2. 一件素纱做成的单衣，又轻又薄，只有48_____重。（克　斤）

3. 唐宋时期，丝织品已是各_____各样，美丽非凡。（式　试）

4. 唐代的一种薄绸，两面有_____，还能透过光线。

（蚊子　花纹）

第五课 丝绸

5. 百鸟羽毛的裙子，正看是一色，_____看是一色。（侧　册）

6. 大约公元前2_____，古罗马人得到了丝绸。（世纪　世界）

7. 丝绸受到了罗马人的_____。（追捧　追赶）

七　根据课文判断对错

1. 丝绸起源于中国，中国也被称为"丝绸之国"。　　　___对___错

2. 甲骨文中有桑、蚕、丝、帛等古文字。　　　　　　___对___错

3. 《诗经》中没有采桑、养蚕的诗歌。　　　　　　　___对___错

4. 丝绸只能做衣服。　　　　　　　　　　　　　　　___对___错

5. 唐代还会用百鸟的羽毛和蚕丝织裙子。　　　　　　___对___错

6. 据说，罗马的恺撒大帝穿过丝绸的袍子。　　　　　___对___错

八　缩写课文（不少于6句）

第五课 丝绸

九 阅读作业

（一）读《绞丝旁》回答问题

绞丝旁

许多带绞丝旁的字与丝绸的生产相关。

比如"缫"丝，就是把茧子放入热水中，找出丝头抽丝。丝很"细"，容易打"结"，"缠"死，"绞"在一起。丝"绕"好后开始"纺""织"。丝绸织好后染色。这些颜色中有"红"色、"绿"色。织出的丝绸品种很多，每个品种都有自己的名字如："绢""纱"等。还有用"线""缝"衣服、"绣"花等。

回答问题

1. 写出你认识的带有绞丝旁的字：_____

2. 写出你不认识的带有绞丝旁的字：_____

（二）读《采桑养蚕》画一幅画儿

采桑养蚕

俗语"养蚕先养桑"，有了桑树蚕就有了"口粮"。中国古来是男耕女织的小农经济，政府重视农桑。战国时期的孟子，认为农家最理想的

第五课
丝 绸

生产和生活是:"五亩地的院落,墙边种满桑树,妇女养蚕;家中有五只母鸡,两头猪;一百亩的农田,男人耕种。"所以中国古代,种桑养蚕,一直是社会生活富足的基础。

画图:画出孟子描述的农民理想生活

提示:房、桑树、鸡、猪、农田等

十　读课文两遍

第七课
扁鹊的四诊法

一 写生词

诊					
扁	鹊				
奠	基				
一	旦				
瘟	疫				
流	行				
驱	鬼				
针	灸				

汤	药				
治	疗				
血	脉				
肠	胃				
骨	髓				
触	摸				
医	疗				
理	论				
经	验				

二 下列汉字是由哪些部分组成的

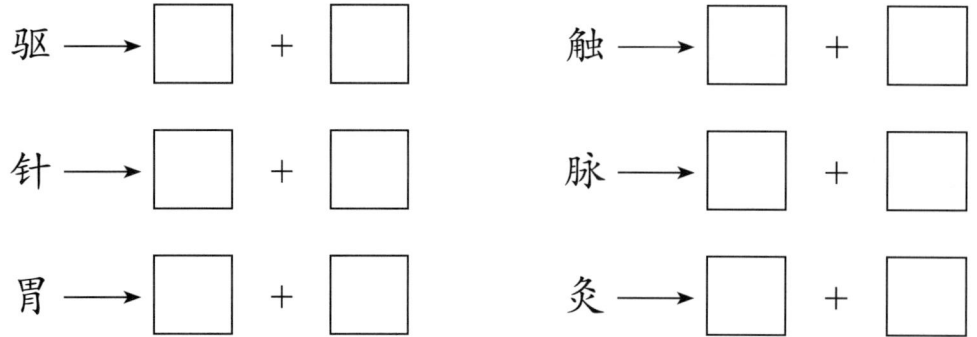

第七课 扁鹊的四诊法

三 组词

门诊　山脉　治病　医疗

诊 { _____
　　_____ }

脉 { _____
　　_____ }

治 { _____
　　_____ }

疗 { _____
　　_____ }

四 写拼音，再组词

温 _____　_____

瘟 _____　_____

五 选择填空

1. 秦越人年轻时，有一年，_____流行，很多人死了。

2. 扁鹊精通_____、_____等各种医术。

3. 扁鹊说蔡桓公有病，病在皮肤，应马上_____。

4. 扁鹊看病主要靠_____：望、闻、问、切。

5. 扁鹊带着他的_____在各地行医。

第七课 扁鹊的四诊法

六 根据课文判断对错

1. 扁鹊是春秋战国时期的一位名医。　　　　　___对___错

2. 扁鹊原来的名字叫秦越人。　　　　　　　　___对___错

3. 那时一有瘟疫流行，国家就请医生驱鬼。　　___对___错

4. 扁鹊见到蔡桓公，说他有病，要马上治疗。　___对___错

5. 蔡桓公相信扁鹊，请他治病。　　　　　　　___对___错

6. 不久蔡桓公果然发病死了。　　　　　　　　___对___错

7. 扁鹊是中医的奠基者之一。　　　　　　　　___对___错

七 将扁鹊的四诊法与适当的解释连线

望　　　　　问病人的情况和病史

闻　　　　　听病人发出的声音，嗅病人身上的气味

问　　　　　触摸病人身体和把脉

切　　　　　看病人脸色、舌头

八 选择填空

1. 扁鹊第一次见到蔡桓公时，说他的病在_____。

2. 扁鹊第二次见到蔡桓公时，说他的病在_____。

3. 扁鹊第三次见到蔡桓公时，说他的病在_____。

第七课
扁鹊的四诊法

4. 扁鹊第四次见到蔡桓公时，说他的病在_____。

5. 不久蔡桓公果然发病_____。

九 造句

一旦_____

经验_____

十 将图中虫子的触角涂上红色

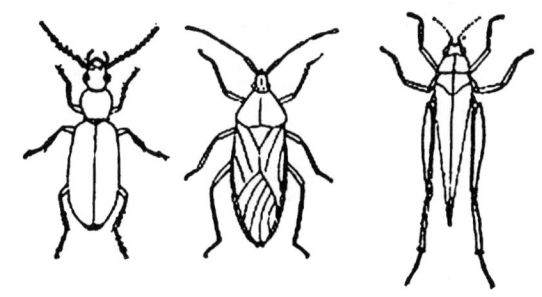

十一 缩写课文（不少于6句）

第七课
扁鹊的四诊法

十二 ‖ 阅读作业 ‖

（一）根据阅读文章《起死回生》判断对错

1. 一次扁鹊在虢国，听说太子刚刚出生。　　　　___对___错
2. 扁鹊赶到王宫，给太子摸脉，还有微脉在跳。　___对___错
3. 扁鹊取针急救，后又用汤药调理，把太子治好了。___对___错

（二）阅读文章《孙思邈》并回答问题

孙思邈

唐代有位著名的医学家叫孙思邈。他医术高明，留下许多救助病人的故事。

一次，有位病人排不出尿，肚子又胀又疼。孙思邈认为吃药已来不及了，要把尿先引出来。他用葱管切去尖的一头，小心插入病人尿道，用力一吸，果然尿液顺着葱管流了出来，病人得救了。又有一次，他在路上看见四个人抬着一口棺材，棺材里流出了鲜血。一问才知是产妇生孩子，两天两夜没生出来，死了。孙思邈说："从这血看，可能没死，让我试试。"棺材被打开了，那妇人脸上已无血色，仔细摸脉，还有一点儿跳

第七课
扁鹊的四诊法

动。他赶忙给病人针灸,不久,产妇醒了过来,孩子也生出来了。一针救了两条命。

老年时,孙思邈将一生行医的经验写成一本书,叫《千金方》。

选择填空

1. 著名医药学家孙思邈是_____的人。

  A. 春秋战国时期　　　　B. 唐代　　　　　　C. 当代

2. 孙思邈用什么办法帮助病人导尿?

  A. 吃药　　　　　　　B. 针灸　　　　　　C. 葱管

3. 孙思邈给一位生孩子的妇女针灸,_____。

  A. 救活了两个人的命　　B. 救活了一个人的命　C. 失败了

4. 老年时孙思邈将一生行医的经验写成一本书叫_____。

  A.《黄帝八十一难经》　B.《千金方》　　　　C.《诗经》

十三　读课文两遍

第九课 都江堰

一 写生词

坝					
亩					
窄					
股					
垒					
瓶					
笼					
昼	夜				

灌	溉				
岷	江				
劈	开				
坚	硬				
冲	垮				
荒	年				
都	江	堰			
水	利	工	程		

二 组新字

石 + 更 → ☐   并 + 瓦 → ☐

土 + 夸 → ☐   尺 + 旦 → ☐

第九课 都江堰

☆ ———— ☆ ———— ☆

活泼　灯笼　一瓶水　股票

三　组词

泼 { _____　　笼 { _____

瓶 { _____　　股 { _____

四　选字组词

回（家　稼）　　姓（张　涨）　　牢（固　国）

庄（家　稼）　　上（张　涨）　　回（固　国）

五　写拼音，再组词

堤 _____　_____　　提 _____　_____

六　反义词

宽—_____　　涨—_____　　硬—_____

七　选择正确的量词填空

股　只　片

一（ 股 ）泉水　　　　一（ 　 ）烟味

第九课 都江堰

八 选择填空

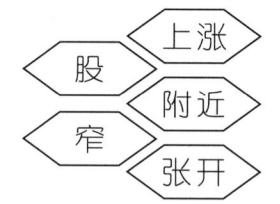

1. 公路_____的森林发生了火灾。

2. 河马_____大嘴时,样子真吓人。

3. 青菜的价钱一直在_____。

4. 打开门,闻到一_____烤肉的香味。

5. 上山的路越走越_____。

九 根据课文选择填空

1. 都江堰是世界著名的_____。

    A. 建筑物   B. 大运河   C. 水利工程

2. 都江堰在中国_____附近。

    A. 上海   B. 河北省赵州   C. 四川省成都市

3. 都江堰是_____修建的。

    A. 战国时期   B. 唐朝

4. 都江堰是秦国的_____修建的。

    A. 李时珍   B. 李冰   C. 李春

第九课 都江堰

十 根据课文判断对错

1. 都江堰建成前，岷江时常发洪水。　　　　　　　___对___错

2. 李冰和百姓看地形，找到了火灾原因。　　　　　___对___错

3. 李冰决定开新河道把水引到成都平原。　　　　　___对___错

4. 李冰带人把玉垒山凿开一个口子，叫鱼嘴。　　　___对___错

5. 建分水堤是用小竹笼放满鹅卵石沉入江里。　　　___对___错

6. 都江堰的内江是老河道。　　　　　　　　　　　___对___错

7. 都江堰的内江水通过宝瓶口，流向成都平原。　　___对___错

8. 都江堰到现在仍在造福成都平原。　　　　　　　___对___错

十一 将方框中词语与合适的解释连线

不分昼夜	世界有名
水旱从人	雨水和干旱由人掌握
闻名世界	不分白天和夜晚

十二 造句

尽管……却……_____

第九课 都江堰

十三 写一写都江堰给你留下的印象（至少8句）

十四 ‖ 阅读作业 ‖

请画一幅都江堰草图，标上右边所列地名

内江　鱼嘴　外江　宝瓶口　飞沙堰

十五 读课文两遍

第一课　听写

1.	2.	3.	4.
5.	6.	7.	8.
9.	10.	11.	12.

第三课　听写

1.	2.	3.	4.
5.	6.	7.	8.
9.	10.	11.	12.

第五课　听写

1.	2.	3.	4.
5.	6.	7.	8.
9.	10.	11.	12.

第七课　听写

1.	2.	3.	4.
5.	6.	7.	8.
9.	10.	11.	12.

第九课　听写

1.	2.	3.	4.
5.	6.	7.	8.
9.	10.	11.	12.

1.	2.	3.	4.
5.	6.	7.	8.
9.	10.	11.	12.

1.	2.	3.	4.
5.	6.	7.	8.
9.	10.	11.	12.

1.	2.	3.	4.
5.	6.	7.	8.
9.	10.	11.	12.

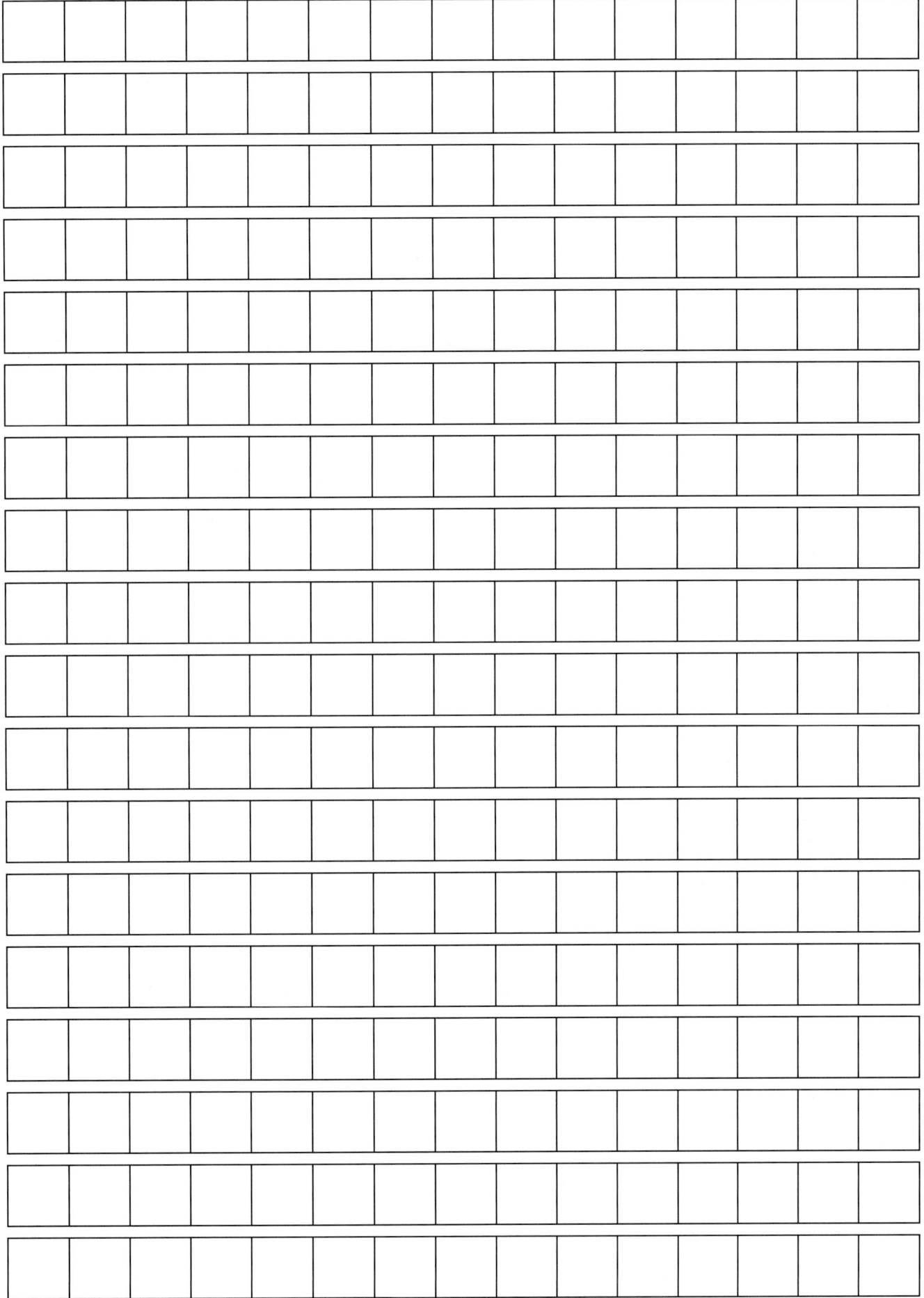

新双双中文教材 10
New Chinese Language and Culture Course

中国古代科学技术 Ancient Chinese Science and Technology

练习本 双课

（第二版）

[美] 王双双 编著

北京大学出版社
PEKING UNIVERSITY PRESS

目　录

第二课　四大发明（二）蔡伦造纸 …………………… 1

第四课　四大发明（四）活字印刷术 …………………… 7

第六课　李春造桥 …………………………………… 12

第八课　李时珍和他的《本草纲目》 …………………… 17

第十课　中国瓷器 …………………………………… 22

第二课
四大发明（二）蔡伦造纸

一 写生词

帛						粗	糙				
麻						棍	子				
揭						丝	绵				
浆						生	产				
墨						渔	网				
蔡	伦					破	布				
竹	简					原	料				
笨	重					试	验				
报	告					理	想				
丝	絮					阿	拉	伯			

二 下列汉字是由哪些部分组成的

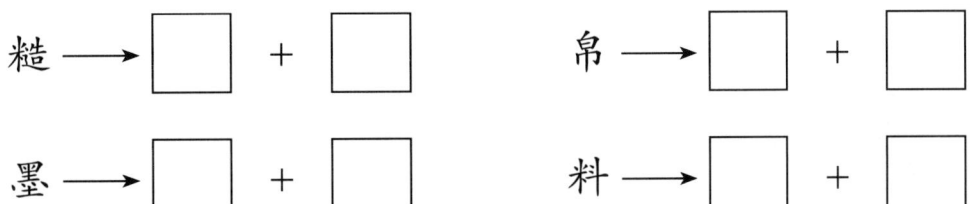

第二课
四大发明（二）蔡伦造纸

三 在方框中圈出词语，再将有相同字的词语放在一组

纸	报	原	便
浆	料	纸	宜
报	告	方	不
豆	浆	便	料

{ 报纸
  报告
{ ⎯⎯⎯
  ⎯⎯⎯
{ ⎯⎯⎯
  ⎯⎯⎯
{ ⎯⎯⎯
  ⎯⎯⎯

四 选字组词

（敲 高）门　　（揭 喝）开　　破（布 巾）

（敲 高）兴　　（揭 喝）水　　毛（布 巾）

五 变换偏旁组成新字，再组词

验 脸 　洗脸　　　　　粗 □ ⎯⎯⎯

棉 □ ⎯⎯⎯　　　　　揭 □ ⎯⎯⎯

2

第二课
四大发明(二)蔡伦造纸

六 圈出下面字的相同部分并写在横线上

| 布 | | 帛 | | 纸 |
| 帛 | | 锦 | | 绸 |

巾
_____   _____   _____

七 写出反义词

便宜—_____   笨重—_____   光滑—_____

八 写拼音

揭 _____   喝 _____   渴 _____

九 选择填空

报告　便宜　粗糙　原料　豆浆　揭

1. 爷爷喜欢早上吃油条，喝_____。

2. 西汉时，已有人用丝絮和麻造纸，但这种纸很_____。

3. 中国制造的玩具又好又_____。

4. 蔡伦把树皮、破布、旧渔网、麻头当作造纸的_____。

5. 絮片_____下来，就可以写字了。

第二课
四大发明（二）蔡伦造纸

十　根据课文判断对错

1. 古代中国人把字写在竹简上，竹简又轻又方便。　　____对____错

2. 古时候，有钱人才能用帛写字。　　____对____错

3. 蔡伦用树皮、麻头、旧渔网、破布造纸。　　____对____错

4. 蔡伦造纸试验了许多次。　　____对____错

5. 蔡伦造的纸又轻又便宜，但是不好用。　　____对____错

6. 公元前105年，蔡伦把这一重大发现报告给皇帝。　　____对____错

7. 造纸术几百年后传到世界各地。　　____对____错

8. 造纸术只促进了中国文化的发展。　　____对____错

十一　造句

便宜_____

生产_____

第二课
四大发明(二)蔡伦造纸

十二 看汉代造纸过程图，写出图画内容

提示：1. 切碎原料在水中泡软　2. 蒸煮原料　3. 捶打原料成纸浆

　　　4. 纸浆放入清水用帘子捞出湿纸　5. 晒干湿纸

_____

_____

_____

_____

_____

十三 ‖阅读作业‖

完成下列句子

纸出现以前，人们把文字写在哪里？

古苏美尔人在_____。

第二课
四大发明（二）蔡伦造纸

古埃及人在_____。

古印度人在_____。

古代欧洲人在_____。

古代中国人在_____。

> 莎草纸上写字
> 兽骨、金属、竹简上刻写文字
> 泥版上刻写文字
> 羊皮纸上写字
> 贝叶上写字

十四 选做题

（一）查找古埃及人用莎草纸的有关资料，并写出来

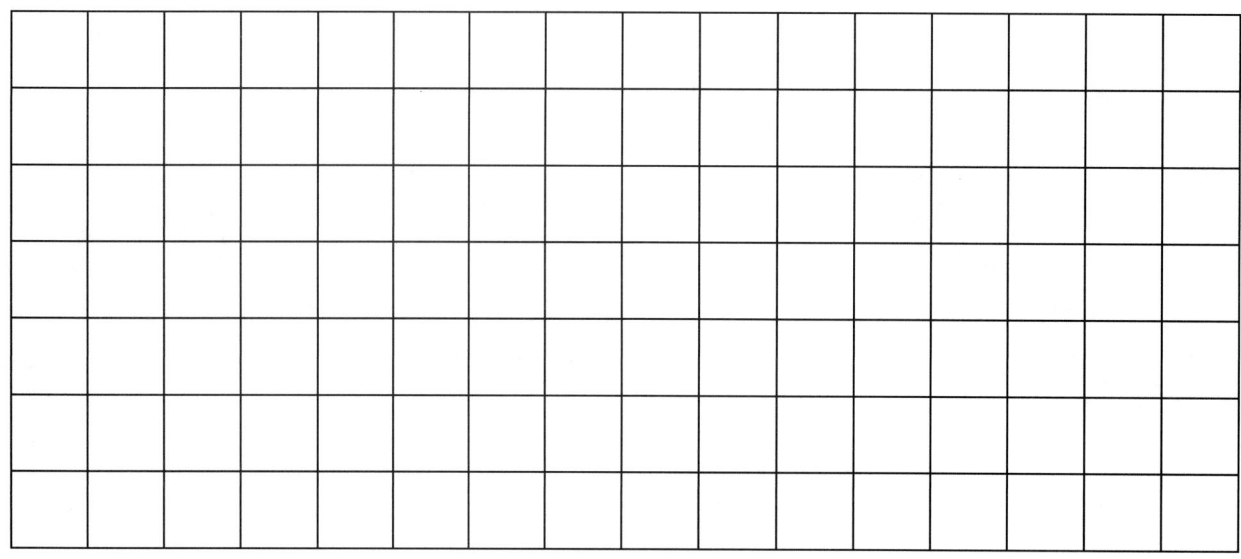

（二）做一张手工纸

十五 读课文两遍

第四课
四大发明(四)活字印刷术

一 写生词

补					
蜡					
粘					
泡					
印	刷				
抄	写				
速	度				
雕	版				

毕	升				
工	匠				
作	废				
拆	开				
胶	泥				
结	实				
稿	件				
压	平				

二 组新字

片 + 反 ⟶ ☐　　月 + 交 ⟶ ☐

米 + 占 ⟶ ☐　　广 + 发 ⟶ ☐

禾 + 高 ⟶ ☐

第四课
四大发明(四)活字印刷术

三 选字组词

（泡 包）茶　　（胶 交）泥　　（稿 高）件

（泡 包）子　　（胶 交）给　　（稿 高）山

四 写拼音

版 _____　　交 _____　　泡 _____
板 _____　　胶 _____　　跑 _____

五 选方框中合适的字组词

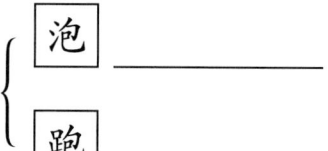

厂_____　　该_____　　泡_____

压_____　　刻_____　　包_____

六 反义词

泡 —— _____　　　　固定 —— _____

第四课 四大发明（四）活字印刷术

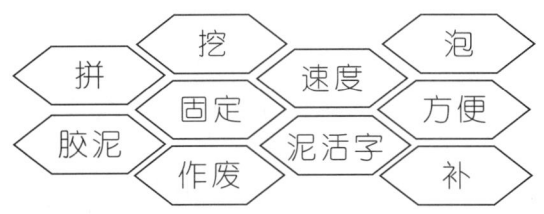

七 根据课文选择填空

1. 中国古代在印刷术发明以前，书要一个字一个字地用手抄写，_____很慢。

2. 雕版印刷比手抄书快，但是每块雕版上的字都是_____在一起的，每换一次内容就得重刻一次版，很不_____。

3. 毕升刻字时，一笔刻坏了，整块版就_____了。

4. 毕升把刻坏的字_____去，再刻一个字_____进去。

5. 毕升用小块木头刻了许多单字，这些字能_____能拆，就叫它"活字"。

6. 几次印刷之后，木活字被水_____得变了形。

7. 小孩子玩的骰子，是用_____烧的，又结实又不怕水。

8. 毕升在胶泥上刻字，做成字印，再用火烧成_____。

八 根据课文判断对错

1. 中国古代在印刷术发明以前，书是用手抄写的。 ___对___错

2. 唐朝初期，人们发明了雕版印刷术。 ___对___错

3. 雕版刻字，一笔刻坏了，整块版就作废了。 ___对___错

第四课
四大发明（四）活字印刷术

4. 北宋人毕升发明了活字印刷术。　　　　　　　　____对____错

5. 泥活字很结实，但是怕水。　　　　　　　　　　____对____错

6. 印刷术后来传到朝鲜、日本、阿拉伯和欧洲。　　____对____错

九 造句

例：王玲不仅喜欢跳舞，也喜欢唱歌。

不仅……也……_____

作废_____

十 阅读作业

根据《印章、拓片与印刷术》选择填空

1. 印章在中国2,000年前的_____时期就有了。（　　）

　　A. 宋朝　　　　　　　　B. 先秦

2. 印章的一般用处是表示_____。（　　）

　　A. 姓名、官职或机构　　B. 活字印刷

3. 碑刻，是将文字刻在_____。（　　）

　　A. 石碑上　　　　　　　B. 木头上

第四课
四大发明（四）活字印刷术

4. 印章和拓片给印刷术提供了_____。（　　）

　　A. 金钱　　　　　　　　B. 直接的经验

十一　选做题：动脑筋想想，印章和单个活字有什么相似之处？写出来

十二　读课文两遍

第六课
李春造桥

一 写生词

弯					
隋	朝				
设	计				
瓦	匠				
师	傅				
请	教				
涨	水				
牢	固				
桥	墩				

拱	形				
结	构				
冲	力				
节	省				
平	缓				
美	观				
地	震				
横	跨				
过	往				

二 下列汉字是由哪些部分组成的

桥 ⟶ ☐ + ☐   固 ⟶ ☐ + ☐

教 ⟶ ☐ + ☐   易 ⟶ ☐ + ☐

第六课 李春造桥

三 组词

观看　缓慢　节日　建设

观 { _____

缓 { _____

节 { _____

设 { _____

四 选字组词

（洪　拱）水　　（至　到）今　　平（缓　爱）

（洪　拱）形　　（至　到）达　　热（缓　爱）

五 写出反义词

弯 — _____　　　　减 — _____

容易 — _____　　　缓 — _____

第六课 李春造桥

六 写拼音

拱形 _____   洪水 _____

七 从"墩"字中能找出几个字？请写出来

墩

☐ ☐ ☐ ☐ ☐ ☐ ☐ ☐

八 选择填空

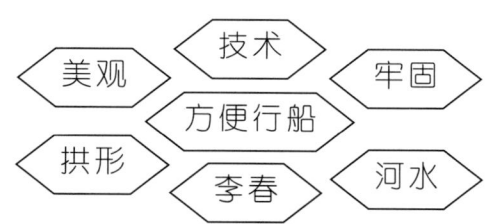

1. 赵州桥是一千多年前，隋朝的石匠_____设计的。

2. 李春从小跟着父亲学习_____。

3. 赵州桥是一座单孔_____石桥。

第六课
李春造桥

4. 发大水时，_____还可以从赵州桥的四个小桥洞流走。

5. 赵州桥的好处有：_____、_____、_____。

九 根据课文判断对错

1. 赵州桥是一千多年前建的一座古桥。　　　　　　　　___对___错

2. 赵州桥是瓦匠李春设计的。　　　　　　　　　　　　___对___错

3. 赵州桥是单孔拱形石桥，方便行船。　　　　　　　　___对___错

4. 经过多次风雨、洪水和地震，赵州桥至今完好。　　　___对___错

5. 赵州桥桥体两边，各开六个小桥洞。　　　　　　　　___对___错

6. 赵州桥桥面平缓，行人和马车过桥都不吃力。　　　　___对___错

十 造句

至今_____

设计_____

第六课
李春造桥

十一 ‖阅读作业‖

写出不同种类桥的编号

梁桥_____   拱桥_____   浮桥_____

索桥_____   梁桥+浮桥_____

十二　读课文两遍

第八课
李时珍和他的《本草纲目》

☆------☆------☆

一 写生词

卷					
纲 目					
家 庭					
错 误					
漏 写					
药 方					
药 渣					
药 铺					
朝 廷					
阅 读					

典 籍					
校 订					
疑 问					
收 集					
科 学					
形 态					
制 作					
附 上					
翻 译					

二 组新字

言 + 吴 → ☐   言 + 卖 → ☐

禾 + 斗 → ☐   太 + 心 → ☐

第八课
李时珍和他的《本草纲目》

三 组词

店铺　修理　附近　漏水

铺 { _____

修 { _____

附 { _____

漏 { _____

四 圈出下列字词

纲目　错误　漏写　药方　药铺　阅读　典籍　疑问
制作　记录　收集　考察　形态　附上　翻译

纲	错	误	附	漏	形	收	集
籍	目	药	态	记	阅	疑	问
错	形	铺	上	录	收	漏	渣
考	掉	误	家	药	纲	集	作
收	方	庭	典	态	方	上	阅
药	渣	附	作	制	渣	读	庭
译	考	察	读	漏	写	翻	铺
察	疑	典	籍	形	集	译	录
附	上	掉	方	态	附	制	误

第八课
李时珍和他的《本草纲目》

五 写拼音

学校 _____　　　校订 _____

六 写出反义词

科学 — _____　　错误 — _____　　疑问 — _____

八 选择填空

1. 李时珍是明代著名的_____学家。

2. 李时珍发现医药书籍中有不少_____和_____之处。

3. 1565年，李时珍带着数不清的_____开始了十年的旅行考察。

4. 李时珍走访了长江、黄河_____和广东、广西等地并采药。

5. 1596年，《本草纲目》_____。

九 根据课文判断对错

1. 李时珍是唐朝人，出生在一个医生家庭。　　___对___错

2. 李时珍看到药书的错误是会害死人的。　　___对___错

3. 李时珍当医官时阅读了大量的医学典籍。　　___对___错

4. 编书前，李时珍收集了大量的实物资料。　　___对___错

第八课
李时珍和他的《本草纲目》

5. 李时珍写《本草纲目》用了37年的时间。　　　___对___错

6.《本草纲目》被翻译成多种文字流传于世界。　　　___对___错

十　将方框中的词语与合适的解释连线

修"本草"	错误和漏掉没写进去的内容
朝廷	修改原有的"本草"药书
错漏	指宫廷、中央政府
医学典籍	重要医学文献

十一　造句

错误_____

阅读_____

十二　‖阅读作业‖

选词填空

1. 疟疾是世界上的一种_____病。

2. 1972年，屠呦呦发现治疗疟疾的药物_____。

3. 2015年，屠呦呦获得诺贝尔_____奖。

第八课
李时珍和他的《本草纲目》

十三 介绍一种你了解的中药材（名称、形态、味道、治什么病）

提示：

生活中常见的中药材：红枣、生姜、枸杞、桂圆等

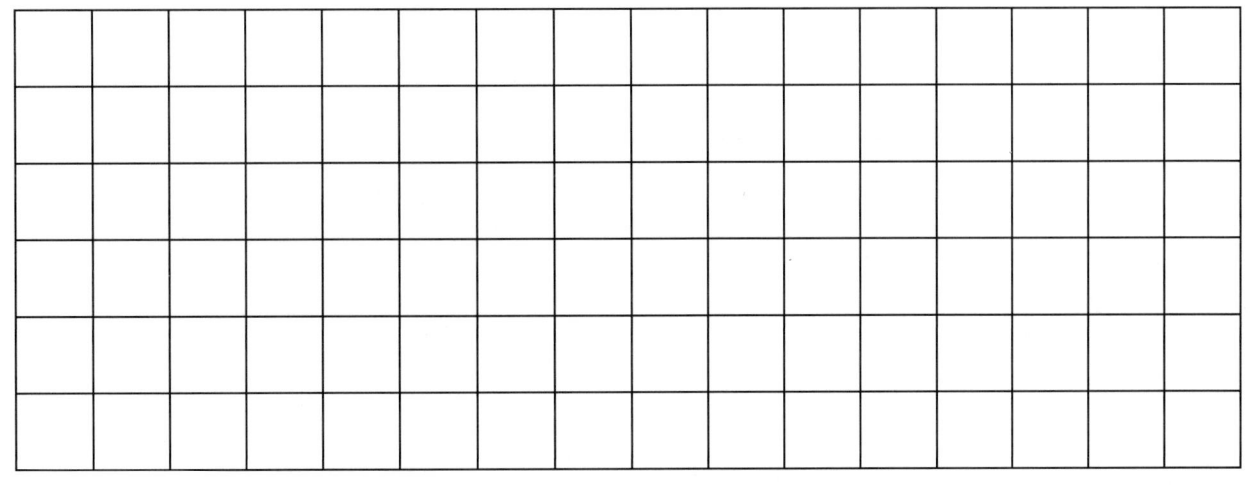

十四 读课文两遍

第十课
中国瓷器

一 写生词

盖					
脆					
胎					
釉					
销					
异					
瓷	器				
厨	房				
客	厅				
厕	所				

马	桶				
瓷	砖				
工	业				
需	要				
陶	器				
原	始				
优	点				
诞	生				
市	场				
题	材				
碰	撞				

二 组新字

次 + 瓦 ⟶ ☐   月 + 危 ⟶ ☐   石 + 专 ⟶ ☐

釆 + 由 ⟶ ☐   女 + 台 ⟶ ☐   石 + 并 ⟶ ☐

月 + 台 ⟶ ☐

第十课 中国瓷器

三 组词

客气　陶器　作业

客 { _____　　业 { _____　　器 { _____

四 选字组词

（次 瓷）器　　（消 销）息　　（危 脆）险

一（次 瓷）　　外（消 销）　　（危 脆）弱

五 写拼音

| 淘气 | _____ |
| 陶器 | _____ |

| 几乎 | _____ |
| 几个 | _____ |

六 写出反义词

优点 — _____　　　　诞生 — _____

第十课 中国瓷器

七 选词填空

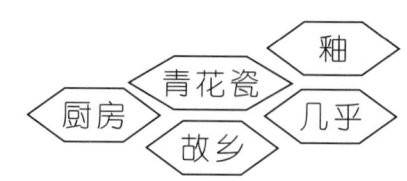

厨房　青花瓷　釉　故乡　几乎

1. 瓷器是中国人发明的，中国是瓷器的_____。

2. 现在人们的日常生活_____离不开瓷器。

3. _____里的瓷盘、瓷碗，厕所里的瓷马桶都是瓷做的。

4. 彩瓷中最有名的是_____。

5. 瓷器是用土做胎，在胎上涂了一种叫_____的东西，再放到1,200度的高温中去烧。

八 选择填空

1. 其实_____上也需要瓷器。

　　A. 工业　　　　B. 作业

2. 很快瓷器就成了世界市场上的_____商品。

　　A. 枪手　　　　B. 抢手

3. 瓷器坚硬，外表光亮好看，不吸水，方便清洗。这些_____是陶器所没有的。

　　A. 优点　　　　B. 缺点

4. 12世纪的宋朝时，中国瓷已销到日本、朝鲜等_____。

　　A. 五个国家　　　B. 五十多个国家

第十课
中国瓷器

☆ ---------- ☆ ---------- ☆

九 根据课文判断对错

1. 瓷器走进人类生活，已有1,800多年了。　　　　　___对___错

2. 三千年前的商朝，中国人发明了"青花瓷"。　　　___对___错

3. 1,800年前（东汉），真正的青瓷烧制出来了。
   这时瓷器才算诞生了。　　　　　　　　　　　　___对___错

4. 明朝之后，中国瓷器通过丝绸之路运往中东
   和欧洲。　　　　　　　　　　　　　　　　　　___对___错

5. 那时中国瓷器虽然很贵，但还是供不应求。　　　___对___错

6. 白瓷很重要，有了白瓷才可以在瓷器上画画儿。　___对___错

7. 青花瓷一出现就受到人们的喜爱。　　　　　　　___对___错

十 仔细看看，家中哪些东西是用瓷做的？请写出来

_____

_____

十一 造句

需要_____

第十课
中国瓷器

十二 ‖ 阅读作业 ‖

（一）根据《瓷行天下——外销瓷》选择填空

    1. 中国瓷器的历史，一定少不了_____。

        A. 外销瓷   B. 外销服装

    2. 明中期以后，外国商人带来欧洲图案定制_____。

        A. 陶器   B. 瓷器

    3. 中国外销瓷器在16—18世纪多达_____。

        A. 三百万件   B. 三亿件

（二）你家中有没有青花瓷？如果有，请描述一下

    提示：瓷器的形状、厚薄、颜色、图案、用途

十三 读课文两遍

第二课　听写

1.	2.	3.	4.
5.	6.	7.	8.
9.	10.	11.	12.

第四课　听写

1.	2.	3.	4.
5.	6.	7.	8.
9.	10.	11.	12.

第六课　听写

1.	2.	3.	4.
5.	6.	7.	8.
9.	10.	11.	12.

第八课　听写

1.	2.	3.	4.
5.	6.	7.	8.
9.	10.	11.	12.

第十课　听写

1.	2.	3.	4.
5.	6.	7.	8.
9.	10.	11.	12.

1.	2.	3.	4.
5.	6.	7.	8.
9.	10.	11.	12.

1.	2.	3.	4.
5.	6.	7.	8.
9.	10.	11.	12.

1.	2.	3.	4.
5.	6.	7.	8.
9.	10.	11.	12.